BY THE PROVERBS 31 MINISTRIES TEAM

clear mind, peaceful heart

PRAYERS AND DEVOTIONS FOR
SLEEPING WELL IN A WORLD FULL OF WORRY

welcome!

THANK YOU FOR YOUR SUPPORT OF PROVERBS 31 MINISTRIES.

You hold in your hands a collection of devotions and prayers written by women just like you, who know what it's like to find anxiety and worry rise as the sun sets. When our homes are quiet, our minds can race. Sleep is elusive. But it doesn't have to be that way.

We've collected stories of God's faithfulness and goodness because we're confident that, through reading God's Word, prayers and the stories of sisters in Christ, you'll remember the true Source of your help, peace and hope. And knowing that, you can rest easy.

Jesus said: "*Look at the birds of the air; they do not sow or reap or store away in barns, and yet your heavenly Father feeds them. Are you not much more valuable than they? Can any one of you by worrying add a single hour to your life?*" (Matthew 6:26-27, NIV).

We pray you experience the love and care of your heavenly Father as you work through the pages of this book.

We've divided this devotional into four sections to help you find a message that speaks to where you are now. As you review the devotions, you'll find some repeated verses. Our editorial team decided to maintain this repetition as is, trusting that God knew ahead of time you might need to hear some truths more than once.

Sleep well,

Your friends at Proverbs 31 Ministries

THOUGHTS ON PRAYER
by Wendy Blight

What lies heaviest on your heart as you lay your head on your pillow? What burdens do you carry that feel like too much to bear? Do overwhelming fear and anxiety steal your peace and joy?

Knowing the reality of life in this world, I'm guessing you found yourself in one of these questions. A few days after my college graduation, I was victimized by a stranger hiding in my apartment. I lived over a decade imprisoned by fear and anxiety, feeling like God had not only abandoned me but forsaken me.

Years after my attack, I shared my testimony at a women's event. After the event, a woman who was a freshman at my university the year of my attack (who I had never met) shared how she and her small group began to pray for me the day they heard of my attack. She showed me the faded pages of her Bible with my name and the year the event happened next to four highlighted verses in Isaiah 62.

These words stood out to me: "... *and you shall be called by a new name that the mouth of the Lord will give*" (v. 2b) and "*You shall no more be termed* **Forsaken** ... *but you shall be called My Delight Is in Her...*" (v. 4a, ESV).

Did you notice the bolded word? Forsaken. The very word I used in my testimony. Tears fell when I saw my name written in ink next to this passage. That God would appoint this day and time for our paths to cross. That He would open the heavens and allow His daughters a peek into His glorious behind-the-scenes handiwork to show us the magnitude, reach and power of prayer.

For so long I thought of prayer as an assigned task. Something I checked off my list.

Oh, friend, I've learned it's so much more. Prayer is an invitation into a faith-deepening, life-transforming journey with the One who knit you together in the secret place. Who knows you by name. Each accepted invitation ushers you into a glorious encounter with the One who calls you His beloved daughter.

And the more we pray, the more we see God at work. The more we see God at work, the more we watch and wait for His hidden handiwork in our lives.

As you begin this journey into prayer, maybe you feel like I did all those years ago. You're angry with God's silence. You feel forgotten and forsaken. Or maybe you're tired of wrestling with your emotions or with strained, exhausting relationships. You're tired of praying the same prayers over and over again.

No matter what you say or pray, nothing works. Nothing changes. You're a tangled mess of emotions, and "why" questions keep tumbling in.

If you're there, let these words sink in. Just as Jesus was with me through that woman's faith-filled prayers, Jesus is with you. He's as near as your next breath. You need only call on His name. *Jesus.*

Jesus invites us to *"Come to me, all you who are weary and burdened, and I will give you rest"* (Matthew 11:28, NIV). He may not fix everything at that moment. But it's an invitation to come and sit with the only One who can give you rest in the middle of the mess.

That, friend, is why we created this for you. Accept our invitation into this prayer journey. Run to the One who is your strength and your shield. (Psalm 28:7) The One who fights for you. (Exodus 14:14) His presence will never leave you. He will never forsake you. (Deuteronomy 31:6)

When troubles weigh heavily on your heart, when burdens feel like too much to bear, remember this as you lay your head on your pillow: Whether your heavenly Father stills the storm or invites you in, He will be with you.

Before you turn the page, pray with me.

Father, thank You for this invitation to pray. I accept Your invitation. Teach me how to pray in new ways. I don't want my prayer life to be a religious ritual. Something I check off my "to do" list. I want more. So much more. I want to pray honest, personal, vulnerable words that connect my heart to Yours. I want to pray with renewed faith and power. I long for powerful and effective prayers that bring results, that honor and glorify You alone and draw me closer to Your heart. May I always remember how valuable I am ... that You bought me with a price. I am Your blood-bought daughter. May I honor You with my heart, mind and body all the days of my life. May I call upon You in times of trouble and find You faithful and true. Place Your angels of protection around me and keep me safe all the days of my life. I ask this in the name of Jesus, believing wholeheartedly You will be faithful to bring what I've asked to pass. And Father, whatever I do in word or in deed, may I do it all for the glory of Your Name. Amen.

TABLE OF CONTENTS

Overcoming Fear and Uncertainty

Daily Obligations and Pressures

Family Concerns

Trusting God During Difficult Times

overcoming fear & uncertainty

___

PRAYERS AND DEVOTIONS FOR SLEEP

WORRY

clear mind,
peaceful
heart

CHOOSING FACT OVER FEELING
Sarah Freymuth

"Be strong and courageous. Do not be afraid or terrified because of them, for the Lord your God goes with you; he will never leave you nor forsake you." **Deuteronomy 31:6 (NIV)**

I wake with a jolt — heart shocked, alert — mind reeling and running a hundred marathons in minutes. The room around me, black like spilled ink, douses my thoughts with slick lies and unreasonable worries. I've been wracked by anxiety for the last few weeks, fallout from the trauma of three ER visits in a month, my husband and me sick with COVID-19, and absolute terror of the unknown.

I can't relax, can't get myself back to sleep for the fear that pushes me awake, taunting that this is all there is, a new way of living that allows me no rest.

In mental anguish, wracked with the worries that stack on top of one another like cement blocks, I blink and call out to God in the night, repeating promises He has given to me:

"In peace I will lie down and sleep, for you alone, Lord, make me dwell in safety" (Psalm 4:8, NIV).

The thoughts don't slow, but somehow His words slip through the stream of scared thinking and my running anxiety. Here, I hold to Him whom I can't see, and He is at work fighting on my behalf. My husband relays this confirmation as we sit in bed and I breathe:

"God is my refuge, my strength, my deliverer."

Over and over, I speak these words, telling myself He is near. He is trustworthy. He is *for* me, and I am His daughter.

Anxiety can paralyze; worry can wrap us in a shroud of dread. But it's here, in the throes of thinking, where we stretch our faith and take stock in a steady God who carries us through our suffering. He is our rhythm that we repeat again and again, following His light in the valley.

When we feel like we can't hold on to anything against our minds, our fears or our worries, we hold to His Word. That's where He meets us.

His Truth flashes in the fog, a beacon guiding us, even in our frantic fears, back to Him.

"*Be strong and courageous. Do not be afraid or terrified because of them, for the* LORD *your God goes with you; he will never leave you nor forsake you.*" (Deuteronomy 31:6)

I will never leave you nor forsake you, His voice whispers once the winds of worry wind down. Though our emotions may say otherwise, Truth holds us secure, an anchor that gives us faith when we cannot see.

He is with us in the storm, in the madness, in the spiral of thought that sends our emotions reeling and our brains off track. Feelings are fickle, but fact stands firm. When faced with "what if?" and "why?" we pull our minds away from the unknown and toward His face. We look for the mini miracles every day — God's manna in the wilderness. We pull them into our arms, give thanks and savor. Even when it doesn't feel like it, God holds us in the palm of His hand and does not let us go.

I will never leave you nor forsake you.

His guarantee. As I lie back down and curl covers over my shoulders, I cling to what I know about Him, scriptures stuck on my lips. I am not alone. He is my assurance. And He makes good on His word.

Father, You say You are with me. Be my Prince of Peace, my steady thoughts, my assurance in the storm. Never will You leave nor forsake me. You are my comfort and safe place. I'm believing this, for You alone let me dwell in safety. In Jesus' Name, Amen.

DWELLING IN SAFETY
Hadassah Treu

"In peace I will lie down and sleep, for you alone, Lord, make me dwell in safety." **Psalm 4:8 (NIV)**

After my husband died unexpectedly, I was unprepared for the multiple losses crushing down on me like mighty, terrifying waves. One of the main losses I experienced was loss of the feeling of safety and security.

My husband made me feel loved, protected and secure. He was my best friend and protector, taking care of me in many different ways. When he died, I suddenly found myself cut off from my future. Instead of a bright future together full of fulfilled wishes and dreams, I found myself staring into a black abyss.

I could not envisage a future for myself.

Losing my feeling of safety and security left me anxious. It seemed that everything in my new life as a fresh widow had the power to send me reeling back in terror. I didn't know one major aspect of grief is struggling with worry and fears — fear about the future being one of the most powerful ones.

This fear was especially harassing me in the evenings when I laid my troubled head on the pillow. I cried to God each night to give me a weapon against this fear. God is faithful, and He often reminded me of this verse: *"In peace I will lie down and sleep, for you alone, Lord, make me dwell in safety"* (Psalm 4:8).

I never thought I could experience this verse on a completely new, deeper level. Breaking this verse into words and phrases, praying and meditating on them, has been an enormous help when I have struggled with fears and uncertainties about the future. Let's break it down together.

"In peace I will lie down and sleep ..." What a mighty declaration of faith! God is faithful to supply peace each night when we struggle to see something good in our future. He is ready to make the exchange: Instead of worry, He gives peace. Instead of exhaustion, He gives rest. Instead of sleepless nights, He blesses us with sleep. But it is on us to trust Him about this and accept His gifts with open hands. It is on us to

take a step of faith and lie down, expecting that He will take care of us by providing a good night's rest.

"... *for you alone,* Lord, *make me dwell in safety.*" What or who makes you dwell in safety? Is it a person or routine? Yes, it is possible that some people in our lives can make us feel safe and secure, but it is not wise to count on them to give us this sense of foundational safety and security we crave. Even routines can make us feel safe, but making them the source of our safety is equally unwise.

The verse tells us that the Lord alone is the source of our safety. Only He can make us dwell in safety. This is the safety and security of His presence and eternal love.

Heavenly Father, thank You, for You alone make me dwell in safety. Please remind me of this truth when I struggle with fears and uncertainties about the future. Thank You for being the blessed controller of my future. You know the end from the beginning and everything in between, and nothing can catch You off guard. My future belongs to You, and You are with me every step of the way. You have ordained every single day of my life, and You have prepared good things for me. That's why, in peace, I will lie down and sleep. In Jesus' Name, Amen.

HOW TO REGAIN A HOPE-FILLED PERSPECTIVE
Laura Lacey Johnson

"But forget all that—it is nothing compared to what I am going to do."
Isaiah 43:18 (NLT)

"Show me your last cool trick!"

With this phrase, my kids knew the time had come to dry off at the swimming pool. They also knew this was their moment to show off and shine. Underwater flips transformed into twirling handstands. Cannonballs became an opportunity to go for gold at the Olympics. I could always expect that the "last cool trick" from yesterday would pale in comparison to what they'd perform today.

Watching my kids made me realize that sometimes I fear God has done His last cool trick in my life. Discouragement convinces me that my best days lie behind me — or that my situation is too complicated or insignificant for God to intervene and do something new. *Sure, God still does great things in other people's lives, just not mine.*

Maybe you've thought something similar. Perhaps God healed you several years ago, but the health crisis staring you down now makes you doubt God could ever do that miracle again. Or maybe God showed up years ago in your marriage in some wondrous way, but fear whispers: *That was then, and this is now.*

When doubt limits our belief about what God can do in the future, we risk developing the same mentality as the people to whom Isaiah prophesied. During the Babylonian captivity, the Jews lived in a foreign land with adversaries who dragged them more than 1,600 miles away from Jerusalem. Yet God gave them a message of hope because He wanted to lift their eyes beyond their current situation.

The Jewish captives had become stuck in the past. For centuries, they dwelled on the parting of the Red Sea and couldn't imagine God doing anything more spectacular. (Isaiah 43:16-17; Exodus 14:21-30)

But God wanted to turn their gaze toward the future. Reflecting on this miraculous event, God declared, *"forget all that—it is nothing compared to what I am going to do"* (Isaiah 43:18). Why would God want them to forget one of the most powerful miracles in their exodus from Egypt?

Because God had something new for them!

"For I am about to do something new. See, I have already begun! Do you not see it? I will make a pathway through the wilderness. I will create rivers in the dry wasteland." (Isaiah 43:19, NLT)

Even when our situation and future look as dry as desert sand, we can remember that, for generations, God has specialized in doing a new thing in wastelands. Fear should never hold our hope hostage. Our situation will change. God will never abandon us.

This week, pay attention anytime you place a lid on a household item: the coffee can, leftovers, the crockpot. Ask yourself, "Where am I putting a lid on my faith?"

We can regain a hope-filled perspective by remembering that God's response to us remains the same today as to the ancient Israelites. God is always doing something new, and we can rest in His proven track record of faithfulness.

Lord, as I lay my head down to sleep tonight, I can relate to the Jewish captives who thought their situation would never change. Thank You for how You've worked in my life in the past, and help me remember that my circumstances never limit Your power. Keep reminding me that You care about my situation and You work on my behalf even when I can't see any evidence yet. Please lift my eyes beyond my current situation. Do a new transformative work in me as I trust in Your faithfulness. In Jesus' Name, Amen.

JESUS MEETS US IN OUR DOUBT
Stephanie Amar

"He got up, rebuked the wind and said to the waves, 'Quiet! Be still!' Then the wind died down and it was completely calm." **Mark 4:39 (NIV)**

I tossed and turned as thoughts shot through my head like debris hurtling through a hurricane. I covered my face with the blanket, wishing it would be enough to protect me from the hit, but it wasn't. The heavy gray clouds of "what ifs" began to fog up my mind until I couldn't think of anything else. The future seemed so uncertain. My fears crushed my faith into a chewed-up mustard seed, and my hope into a speck of dust.

At first, my worries were realistic scenarios, and then they became pure overreactions and fantasies. Things that most probably wouldn't happen. But they were enough to keep me up all night with my heart in a knot.

Do you feel the same tonight? Are your fears and uncertainties about the future keeping you up? Take heart, friend, because Jesus meets us right in the middle of our doubt. Jesus meets us exactly where the waves of anxiety rise and the winds of terror knock us down. He calms our raging thoughts and emotions, leaving us in perfect peace.

As I lay in bed, restless, I remembered when Jesus rescued His apostles when their faith was battered by a terrifying storm. After an exhausting day of teaching and miracles, Jesus told them, *"Let us go over to the other side"* of the lake (Mark 4:35, NIV). As they traveled across the lake, a threatening gale hit them. It was so fierce that the disciples, some being veteran fishermen, were sure they were going to die. Thus, their hearts filled with uncertainty and despair. Suddenly, getting to the other side seemed impossible.

As the winds and the water tossed and turned them, Jesus was sound asleep. So the disciples cried out to Him with frustration, thinking He was unaware of their circumstances. But they had every reason to believe Jesus was still in control. After all, they had a front-row seat to Jesus' miracles.

Despite their disbelief, *"He got up, rebuked the wind and said to the waves, 'Quiet! Be still!' Then the wind died down and it was completely calm"* (Mark

4:39). Notice that Jesus didn't abandon them. Jesus didn't walk out and leave them in despair. Their faith was demolished, yet Jesus met them amid the storm and calmed it. They complained, not understanding that He allowed this for their own good. Nonetheless, He tenderly mended their faith when confronting them about their disbelief.

Rest assured that Jesus meets us right where we are tonight. Here in our beds, filled with anxiety about tomorrow's outcome. Struggling to believe that He is more significant than our problems. Indeed, just as He calmed the disciples' turbulence and gave them tranquility by grace, the Lord desires to bring us spiritual peace. So let us go confidently to God, presenting Him with our raging thoughts, emotions and futures, confident He will bring peace and quiet to our hearts.

Lord, my soul and body are exhausted and weary. I yearn for rest but cannot sleep. My future is fogged up with uncertainty. My mind feels like a hurricane of "what ifs." Lord, I am so scared. The outcome is out of my control, and that terrifies me. But I believe that You are Lord even over my worry. Please meet me here in my doubt and anxiety. Please help me rest tonight, trusting that You will be enough for tomorrow. Strengthen my faith. Help me be confident that when the waves rise higher, Your faithfulness will be greater. In Jesus' Name, Amen.

IN THE ARMS OF THE KEEPER
Linda Seabrook

"In peace I will both lie down and sleep; for you alone, O Lord, make me dwell in safety." **Psalm 4:8 (ESV)**

The sound of the front door closing still echoes in my mind. It was all so final. The furniture was in place. The cupboards were filled. The beds were made. The empty boxes were stacked neatly by the door. The last person who had come to my rescue had finally left. Moving day was officially over.

In fact, it felt as if everything was over.

Over the last four months, I had watched my 15-year marriage dissolve in front of my eyes. To be closer to family, I packed up my little life in a minivan and, along with my daughters, moved back to the city where I grew up.

Single parenting, job searching, divorce papers and so much uncertainty seemed to be what lay ahead of me. Every day was another battle to navigate the many emotions that threatened to rule my heart. One moment I was full of worry. The next moment I was overcome with anger. It was all too much for me to take in.

As I crawled into bed later that night, the lonely shadows were just another reminder that this was my new normal. Everything around me seemed calm and sleepy, but my heart was anything but restful. The prayer I said at bedtime over and over as a child now cut me to the core: *As I lay me down to sleep, I pray the Lord my soul to keep.*

More than ever before, I truly needed to know I was kept. I was held. I was loved.

In that moment, these ancient words filled my thoughts: *"In peace I will both lie down and sleep; for you alone, O Lord, make me dwell in safety"* (Psalm 4:8). God was there with me, in my anxiousness and fear, even when life seemed at its darkest.

David, who wrote those words, was a man who experienced his share of difficulties. He was an up-and-coming ruler whom King Saul longed to see dead. Later, family dysfunction and blatant sin brought

David to his knees in despair. Yet despite all the struggles that were woven throughout his story, David could cry out to God in faith. Why? He knew the source of his peace, trust and hope.

David knew the Keeper of his soul.

I have learned through my own days of uncertainty that there is no better place to be than securely resting in the arms of my heavenly Father. Life can be unpredictable. Relationships can devastate. Circumstances can overwhelm. Yet God remains unchanging throughout all of it. His faithfulness reminds me that He can bring calm to the chaos.

Over 15 years have passed since that first night in my new home. It wasn't the only time I have lain awake, wondering and worrying about tomorrow. Yet there is an indescribable peace that comes when I admit to God my worries are much too great a burden for me to bear. Like a little child, weak and needy, I pray for the security of His presence. I pray for the assurance that He is in control. I pray for the One who holds the world in His hands to be the Keeper of my soul.

And He has never failed me yet.

Faithful heavenly Father, when uncertainty seems to cloud my day, I pray for Your blessed rest to pour over my soul tonight. Thank You that Your mercies are new every morning. I surrender my worry to You in exchange for Your peace. I trust You to be my Keeper. You alone are faithful, compassionate, good and worthy of my worship. In Jesus' Name, Amen.

HOPE TO WALK FORWARD
Bonnie Dorough

"I sought the Lord, and He heard me, And delivered me from all my fears." **Psalm 34:4 (NKJV)**

As the obstetrician's nurse left the room, I was alone with my thoughts and a strap across my second-trimester belly to monitor my baby's heart rate and movement. Tears dropped onto my hospital gown, and my mind headed straight for the worst.

I need this baby to live. I can't lose another child. Please, God, I need Your help. I want to trust You.

There are moments when our faith wrestles with fear.

What if something is wrong with my baby? How will I handle that?

Guilt came over me for even thinking those things. I wanted to trust God. I'd experienced God's help in the past, so why couldn't I trust Him now?

It's common to have one foot forward, ready to believe in God's goodness, and the other foot stuck in the cement of the past. The good news is: God can break up that cement and release us from the fears that hold us down. He can ignite hope in the driest soul.

Maybe things didn't work out as we had hoped. Maybe we lost someone or something. Even during grief, there is a battle to believe in God's goodness again for our future — to stand up amid the tears and seek the heart of a Father who loves us.

In Psalm 34:4, David pronounced: *"I sought the Lord, and He heard me, And delivered me from all my fears."* All my fears. That's a pretty tall order, but if anyone can do it, God can.

We can seek the Lord through prayer or worship or just by sitting quietly in His presence. God hears us and delivers us. Our stress can be silenced in the presence of His promise. That is how we participate in God's healing process. We show up, and He does the work. We bring in fear, and He breathes out hope.

There is no fear too big for Him to handle. No thought too dark that He cannot soothe. He sees our tears and knows our fears. He longs to deliver and transition us from past fear to forward faith. Over the years, God faithfully continues to peel fear layers off of me like an onion. As each layer sheds, I discover new hope and confidence in Him.

I chose to give my daughter the middle name Hope because, even after a previous loss, the Lord birthed hope within me.

My daughter recently celebrated her ninth birthday, and I was reminded that our trust in God is never wasted. His help and hope set our feet on new paths away from the cement and into green pastures.

God, I want to walk away from everything I fear, and I need Your help. I don't want to walk this path alone. Your Word says that You will never leave me, that You always hear me and that all things will work out for my good. I ask You to break off the fear that slows me down and instead birth hope deep within me. Help me spring forward into a promising hope for my future. In Jesus' Name, Amen.

SURRENDER IN THE VALLEY
Avril Occilien Similien

"Then God said, 'Take your son, your only son, whom you love—Isaac—and go to the region of Moriah. Sacrifice him there as a burnt offering on a mountain I will show you.'" **Genesis 22:2 (NIV)**

There was a shift in the atmosphere at work. I couldn't quite place my finger on it, but the environment was different. This was my dream job and an answer to prayer when I was at my wit's end. God had promised me He would provide, and He did.

Now, after 11 years, God was calling me to walk away. To leave the security of a salary and follow Him into the unknown.

Not wanting to be duped by my tendency to get bored and seek change, I prayed about it. I sought God's face. Yet as I prayed, I found myself sinking into a low place. I felt like I was caught in a valley — the valley of decision.

How appropriate. For isn't a valley a low place in the land between two hills or mountains? God was calling me from one mountaintop to another, and I felt lost in between.

My mind wandered to the Bible for examples of those also caught in a valley — caught between preserving the promise and walking out their faith in obedience. Abraham came to mind.

God promised Abraham and his wife, Sarah, a son. After Abraham and Sarah spent many years waiting, Isaac was born. One day, God instructed Abraham, *"Take your son, your only son, whom you love—Isaac—and go to the region of Moriah. Sacrifice him there as a burnt offering on a mountain I will show you"* (Genesis 22:2).

In obedience, Abraham took Isaac on a three-day journey to the place of sacrifice. This journey served as Abraham's valley. I wonder what thoughts, questions and doubts may have agonized Abraham in this low place. Still, he pressed on.

As Abraham strapped his son to the altar and raised his weapon in full commitment to surrendering the promise, God intervened and provided a ram as an alternate sacrifice.

Seeing that God had provided, "Abraham called that place The LORD Will Provide. And to this day it is said, 'On the mountain of the LORD it will be provided'" (Genesis 22:14, NIV).

I heard God whisper in my heart, *It's not about the circumstance. It's about the surrender.*

At that moment, I was reminded that God is not only concerned about our actions — He is concerned about our hearts. God gently shifted my focus from the difficult decision before me to the unseen work He was doing within.

Friend, I'm not sure if you are currently in a valley of decision. If you are, I pray that, despite your agonizing thoughts, questions and doubts, you will have the courage to surrender and allow God to do the deep work in the low place.

Not only did Abraham praise God for providing in his current situation, but he also declared God would continue to provide.

As you surrender in the valley, may you be reminded that, no matter what decisions you face or how impossible your circumstances seem, God will provide, just as He promised.

God, I thank You for being a provider. I thank You that my difficult circumstances do not change the promises You have spoken in Your Word. I pray that, as I wrestle with this difficult decision before me, I will have the courage to surrender to the work You are doing in my heart. In Jesus' Name, Amen.

A ROOM WITH A VIEW
Calista Baker

"Lord, you alone are my inheritance, my cup of blessing. You guard all that is mine. The land you have given me is a pleasant land. What a wonderful inheritance!" **Psalm 16:5-6 (NLT)**

It was a picture-perfect morning. Wispy clouds. The yard was a palette of greens with sunspots and shade. The slightest trace of autumn rust and yellow were winking at me through the leaves. I settled into my overstuffed chair, steaming coffee close at hand, with my Bible, journal, gel pens and cat — I was ready. This view from my sunroom is one I love, and this place is one where I meet regularly with God. However, in a few more weeks, after I moved, it wouldn't be my view any longer.

With that realization, melancholy oozed its way in, and contentment was tainted with fear that my new view wouldn't be nearly as lovely. The peace I had experienced just moments ago turned into worry about the upcoming move. My readiness to settle in and hear from God quickly turned into anxious questions about what I was even doing with my life. Please tell me I'm not the only girl who tends to walk hand in hand with melancholy and melodrama.

I took a few minutes to absorb the beauty of my yard along with accompanying memories of the children playing whiffle ball and hunting Easter eggs. I smiled, recalling leaf piles as big as cars, and glittering snow like an acre of diamonds.

Sighing, contented and a little sad, I sensed God whispering to me. He assured me that, as lovely as this view is, I would get a new one, which would have things about it that would be lovely as well. He reminded me that, just as He created the view of my yard from the sunroom, He also created the view from the living room window of my apartment.

I began to understand that what I was experiencing was less about a lovely view than it was my fear of what life would hold for me in the future. The move was a result of a relationship change I had hoped would turn out differently. My life was changing drastically and quickly. There were many unknowns and complications. I was excited and scared.

Psalm 16 says, *"Lord, you alone are my inheritance, my cup of blessing. You guard all that is mine. The land you have given me is a pleasant land. What a wonderful inheritance!"* (Psalm 16:5-6).

God helped me remember He has provided for all my needs. He made everything I see. My view would change, but my God would never change. He still loved me. He would be present with me in my new home with the new view He made for me to enjoy.

The changes in your life, big or small, can bring to the surface all sorts of fear disguised as melancholy goo. Remember that God, the Creator of the universe, knows you and the little things that bring you pleasure — like, maybe, a lovely view. And He is more than able to provide not only what you need but what you enjoy. He is with you where you are today, and He will be with you where you are tomorrow.

Dear God, You are all I need, and because of You I am content to see and enjoy what You provide for me. Thank You that, in all the changes, You never change. And even in the middle of big changes, You make sure I can still see You. Truly, what You have given me is pleasant because You made it all! Thank You for going with me and leading me. Heavenly Father, I trust You always to take care of the details. Nothing escapes Your loving notice. You are faithful, and You are good to me. In Jesus' Name, Amen.

PEACE OF MIND WHEN YOUR FUTURE IS UNKNOWN
Nicole Arbuckle

"You will keep the mind that is dependent on you in perfect peace, for it is trusting in you." **Isaiah 26:3 (CSB)**

My eyes opened to the black of night. I rolled over to look at the clock. It was 2:30 a.m. Could yesterday's news be erased? *Jesus, please work a miracle. Lord, please change the decision. God, why did You allow this to happen?*

Tears rolled down my face as my aching heart started to run through the lists of unknowns regarding our family's future. *Where will we live? How will this affect my kids? What can I do to fix it?*

I could barely breathe.

As I lay in the dark, I could feel my heart beating through my chest. My mind was flooded with fears, and my heart was overwhelmed by uncertainties. *Why don't they want us? Why did he make that decision? I don't want to leave.* My mind raced for the next two hours until I was beyond exhausted and fell back asleep.

We have two choices when our circumstances are heartbreaking, overwhelming and out of our control: We can stay stuck in our sorrow, or we can trust in God's sovereignty.

As I spent time processing, grieving and sitting in the pain, Jesus met me through His Word. He met me in my pain and whispered to my spirit, *Trust Me.* He knew this day would come. He knew what would happen tomorrow. He knew what six months from now would look like. I was only seeing a glimpse of His plan and purpose for my life. I could trust Him.

In times of unknowns and uncertainties, it is easy to obsess over the circumstance. It is hard to see past it. Our natural inclination is to worry about the future, wondering where we will end up and what it all means.

God doesn't want us to focus on our circumstances; He wants us to fixate on Him. He wants us to see our situation through His lens and trust Him.

This is easier said than done.

As I've worked through my anxiousness with my therapist, she has recommended some breathing techniques that I've adapted. I do this in the midst of the days and nights when my heart is beating fast and my breath is shallow.

Breathe.

Don't just breathe in oxygen. Breathe in God's breath: His Word.

Inhale a promise from His Word. Hold it in your mind and breathe for five seconds. Exhale His promise. Repeat it five times.

If your mind needs peace, breathe in these words from Isaiah 26:3 (inhale and hold for five seconds): *"You will keep the mind that is dependent on you in perfect peace ..."* Exhale: *"... for it is trusting in you."*

Here are Bible verses to breathe in as we encounter anxiousness in dealing with unknowns:

- Proverbs 3:5–6: *"Trust in the LORD with all your heart, and do not rely on your own understanding; in all your ways know him, and he will make your paths straight."* (CSB)

- Isaiah 41:10: *"Do not fear, for I am with you; do not be afraid, for I am your God. I will strengthen you; I will help you; I will hold on to you with my righteous right hand."* (CSB)

- Jeremiah 17:7: *"Blessed is the man who trusts in the LORD, whose trust is the LORD."* (ESV)

- Matthew 11:28: *"Come to me, all of you who are weary and burdened, and I will give you rest."* (CSB)

You will make it through this, friend. You are not alone. Breathe deeply. Experience God's presence and peace through the breath of His Word.

Jesus, I don't understand, but I trust You. I trust You are in control. Fill my mind and heart with the peace of Your presence. In Jesus' Name, Amen.

DWELLING IN THE PAUSE
Bethany Heard

"He who dwells in the secret place of the Most High Shall abide under the shadow of the Almighty." **Psalm 91:1 (NKJV)**

I love the pause button on our TV remote. It gives me the illusion that I can control time. Just press "pause" and I can answer the door, make a cup of tea, finish that conversation, then press it again, and I'm right back where I left off.

I have, however, found that I'm not a fan of the pause button being used in my life — especially when I'm not the one who presses it. The last couple of years have felt like one long pause. Time is ticking, and life is swirling around, but my circumstances and my faith have ground to a halt, like a heavy steam locomotive pulling in to the station.

And what's worse is I haven't always made the best use of my pause. I've filled it with thoughts on the past, finding regrets and failures. And I've found many. I've focused so much on the hope of situations changing that I've missed the Savior who is sustaining me. I've allowed doubts and despair to overshadow me.

Yet despite my faithlessness, God is faithful, and the Holy Spirit speaks straight into my pause: *"He who dwells in the secret place of the Most High Shall abide under the shadow of the Almighty"* (Psalm 91:1).

This verse speaks of dwelling in a secret place. My thoughts on "dwelling" have always taken me to quaint little cottages with cozy fires. But when life didn't feel comfortable I began to question where God was in my dwelling.

I recently discovered that, in engineering, the word "dwell" means "a brief pause in the motion of a part of a mechanism to allow an operation to be completed."

I had imagined God dwelling in crackling fires and wooly blankets, but He also dwells in my empty, silent pauses. In fact, He is the One who presses "pause" so He can create a space to work in my life. The pause is necessary. My two-year pause to "dwell" does not feel brief, as defined by the engineers. But in the light of eternity, it is exactly that.

It is in this secret, hidden place, with my life on hold, that God is filling me with His presence and His purpose. The shadows that I'm dwelling in are from Himself. They are His protection over me. In the darkness when all seems still, God is in fact working to complete what He is doing in me.

This is my dwelling. This is my resting place.

In the most significant pause in history, God accomplished His greatest work. As Christ hung on the cross and cried out, *"My God, my God, why have you forsaken me?"* (Matthew 27:46, ESV), darkness fell, and heaven was silent. Jesus' work was finished. All our sins, faults and failures were paid in full in that pause.

My pause is not punishment, nor is it because I've been forgotten; it is because I need completing.

My pause may be out of my control, but instead of looking at the darkness and seeing emptiness, I'm seeing the shadows of His love, and a place for me to dwell.

Father, in my doubts and disappointments, in my life that doesn't seem to be moving forward, may You help me to see that You have allowed this pause as an opportunity to work out what You have begun in me. May You fill this silent, empty space with more of Your presence. May I not wrestle with regrets in the past, and may I not set my hopes on my expectations for my future. Lord, help me to rest in the knowledge that You are using this pause to dwell with me in secret. In Jesus' Name, Amen.

HE LEFT US WITH PEACE – NOT PIECES
Cassidy Poe

"'Peace I leave with you; my peace I give to you. Not as the world gives do I give to you. Let not your hearts be troubled, neither let them be afraid.'" John 14:27 (ESV)

I opened my eyes and there I was: still in the hospital room, wearing a thin green gown with little blue polka dots. The sterile smell lingered in the air as wires emerged from every possible part of my body.

It had been three days. The 64 electrodes attached to my head clearly gave away that something wasn't functioning normally — no matter how many tests came back saying so. I was lying in a hospital bed, unable to walk.

What I didn't know as I lay there praying for answers was that this was just the beginning of a journey that won't end on this side of eternity unless God chooses to miraculously heal me.

At 14, I began having mysterious episodes where I collapsed and had temporary paralysis throughout my body, followed by seizures. As my quest for answers turned from months into years, a dark cloud of constant unknowns taunted my dreams and hopes for the future.

As I have become older, even now as an adult, it has been easy for the uncertainty to take hold of my heart. How do I make plans for next month or next year when tomorrow feels so fickle? What will life look like for me if my body cannot function well?

There is something about the unknown that pulls us, without invitation, into a cycle of fear. We cannot see ahead. We cannot make solid plans. We grow afraid to hope because unfulfilled hope feels more painful than anything we've gone through before.

But in the middle of the fear, anxiety, unknowns and hopes deferred, there is an invitation that beckons us: "*Peace I leave with you ...*" (John 14:27a).

It's an invitation that seems almost too good to be true when we are right in the middle of our struggle. But I love that Jesus says, "*my peace I give to you. Not as the world gives do I give to you*" (John 14:27a-b).

That 14-year-old girl in the hospital room was waiting for peace to be served up on the platter of a diagnosis. Little did I know that there is a much deeper peace that is not dependent on our circumstances.

Jesus could have left us in the shattered pieces of our brokenness. He could have left us in our fear. Jesus could have looked at everything He was about to endure on our behalf and could have chosen to leave us to our own defenses. Instead, He said, *"Peace I leave with you; my peace I give to you"* (John 14:27a). A peace rooted in the unchanging character and sovereignty of God.

As we close our eyes tonight, whether we find ourselves in a stuffy hospital room or with a million worries holding space in our heart — let us cling to Jesus and His invitation: *"Let not your hearts be troubled, neither let them be afraid"* (John 14:27c).

Father God, thank You so much for who You are. Thank You that the uncertainty that lies ahead of me is not unknown to You. You have already gone before me, and You beckon me to take hold of Your peace. So I lift up my struggles to You right now and ask that You bring my heart to peace — peace that can only be found in You. I can rest knowing that You are still moving and working, even when I cannot see it right now. I can be confident in the promises that You will never leave me nor forsake me. Thank You for all You are doing. In Jesus' Name, Amen.

daily obligations & pressures

PRAYERS AND DEVOTIONS FOR SLEEP

IN A WORLD OF WORRY

clear mind,

peaceful

heart

A STACK OF FAILURES AND A GOD WHO SEES OUR HEARTS
Nichole Suvar

"But the Lord said to Samuel, 'Do not look on his appearance or on the height of his stature, because I have rejected him. For the Lord sees not as man sees: man looks on the outward appearance, but the Lord looks on the heart.'" 1 Samuel 16:7 **(ESV)**

I lie in the dark, the feeling of failure weighing heavy. My mind begins to think through the day, taking note of everything I didn't get done.

My efforts feel insignificant. Obligations where I continue to fall short stack up like a burdensome pile of books on my chest. It causes my breathing to shorten, and I stare at the ceiling as tears silently fall.

Maybe you've been there, too. Convinced you are doing nothing that matters; therefore, you do not matter. The weight of failure robs you of sleep, and you toss and turn as your mental list of deficiencies grows. Why do we classify things as failures? Why does our lack of grand accomplishments make us think we got nothing done? Even if we do have an entire day where we got nothing done — why does that matter?

When did we start believing we are the sum of our accomplishments and our production? It happens when we focus on who we are instead of *whose* we are.

God needed to remind the prophet Samuel of this, too, when Samuel was looking to anoint the next king of Israel. Samuel was sure the next king would be one of the taller, stronger, more mature sons of Jesse. When God said "no" to the whole lineup, He reminded Samuel of this truth:

"But the Lord said to Samuel, 'Do not look on his appearance or on the height of his stature, because I have rejected him. For the Lord sees not as man sees: man looks on the outward appearance, but the Lord looks on the heart'" (1 Samuel 16:7).

The same goes for us, too. We live in a world that glorifies the grand, big and amazing. The stranger who becomes a YouTube sensation, the neighbor who writes a book that reaches No. 1 on the bestseller list, and the seemingly random person who makes a Facebook video that goes viral.

When these things happen to normal, everyday people, exciting things feel possible for us, too. So when life moves at a normal, even mundane, pace, we might feel as though, if we aren't grand, we aren't anything.

David was a shepherd. He devoted his entire day just to keeping sheep alive. We could look at a simple life like that and see insignificance. But God knew David's heart, and He chose him as king.

God sees us differently from how the world does. God doesn't look at us as the sum of our accomplishments. Our God looks at the heart. We are made in His image to reflect His glory.

We were chosen to love and share His goodness. If each day we are walking in God's Truth, taking steps toward what He has called us to do and remaining faithful, then we are exactly where we are supposed to be. Perhaps a few of us are called to lead thousands, but more of us are called to lead a few. Those few may have sticky hands, endless jabber and eyes that reflect our genes. Our numbers do not matter, but our faithfulness does.

Heavenly Father, today I feel like I didn't get anything done, and yet the demands on my time and energy don't stop. I want to feel like I'm accomplishing something meaningful for Your Kingdom. Help me see my daily responsibilities as You see them. Help my heart focus more on loving and reflecting Your goodness than making a name for myself or checking more off my to-do list. In Jesus' Name, Amen.

EXCHANGING ANXIETY FOR REST
Susan Mcilmoil

"It is in vain that you rise up early and go late to rest, eating the bread of anxious toil; for he gives to his beloved sleep." **Psalm 127:2 (ESV)**

My tumultuous relationship with sleep began during the time that was, as I see it, the fracturing of my mind. I was newly married in my early 20s, working full time for five attorneys and holding the weight of the world on my shoulders. So much to prove with so little time.

I was already prone to anxiety, so my overburdened mind and body were fertile ground for anxiety and depression's hostile takeover.

Once these two unwelcome guests had settled into my life, nighttime was the most challenging part of my day. The setting sun allowed the shadows of all the "what ifs" to loom far greater. And my husband's tranquil breathing was a reminder that all the world rested while I lay awake clutching my fears.

What if something terrible happens? Who will defend me when I am utterly defenseless? The questions raged as the thoughts overwhelmed, and I stayed awake.

I imagine that Solomon, the author of Psalm 127, had endured a few sleepless nights of overthinking before he concluded that it was useless, writing in verse 2, *"It is in vain that you rise up early and go late to rest, eating the bread of anxious toil; for he gives to his beloved sleep."*

The KJV uses the words *"eat the bread of sorrows."* The Hebrew noun and verb in this little group of words have the meaning of *actively feeding* on hardship, pain, grief, offense or sorrow.

Yes, I was in a season of anxiety, but I had to be painfully honest with myself — I was choosing to actively chew on my sorrows. Instead of succumbing to sleep, which I so desperately needed, my mind ran wild with horrific scenarios.

I wasn't fighting fear and anxiety; I was feeding it and losing precious sleep.

God created us to need rest, and He designed limitations into our frames. Not as a cruel restriction, as my anxious mind would have me believe, but like Psalm 127 says, as a gracious gift. God knew well that His feeble creations would forget their limits and attempt a power grab. Every. Day. So, at the end of every day, He cleverly designed us to become inactive and surrendered.

Of all the things God has given, rest is the one that is most dear to my heart. It becomes that much more precious when it is hard to come by. Because of this, the simple act of sleeping has become a gesture of worship for me. When I lay my worries and my head down, I acknowledge I am not God. Resting says I agree with the psalmist who tells us God is in control, and whatever may or may not happen is in His hands. Sleep is necessary for our bodies, and it can be an act of worship when our perceived control is exchanged for rest.

Friend, never forget you are His beloved, and He gives you the gracious gift of rest. Your fears matter to Him, so be brave and humbly hand them over to the One who can handle holding them.

Father, You say I am Your beloved, and You give me sleep. Help me to believe this truth tonight so I may rest my weary mind and heart. Hold my worries and give me the strength to leave them in Your arms even as I awake. In Jesus' Name, Amen.

PEACE, BE STILL
Rhonda Clark

"And he arose, and rebuked the wind, and said unto the sea, Peace, be still. And the wind ceased, and there was a great calm."
Mark 4:39 (KJV)

My mind is often like my computer with several tabs or windows open all the time. A great visual of this is a juggler keeping multiple balls in the air all at once. More than one thought or idea is always rolling around in my mind.

With this kind of brain, daytime brings many distractions. There's always some task needing my attention — or I can pour my heart out in a writing project. The television and radio can also bring needed disruptions to my thoughts. But in the stillness of the night, no external distractions exist.

So, in the silence of the dark, my brain kicks into high gear. Items for tomorrow's to-do list invade my mind. Previous regrets bubble to the surface, filling me with guilt or shame. Some important detail I neglected to tell my husband 10 different times today is added to the top of tomorrow's list. Meal planning for the days ahead, and on and on and on. You get the idea.

Many times, I've screamed *STOP* inside my brain and pulled the brake on the runaway thought train. This allows my mind to empty, and I can redirect my thoughts to God and His Word. When I force my mind to stop spinning, it's something like when Jesus calmed the storm.

Mark 4:36-41 recounts the story of Jesus sleeping in a boat when a storm was tossing it around. In terror, the disciples awakened Jesus and told Him they were about to sink. Jesus didn't get excited or rush around; He simply got up and quieted the wind and water:

"And he arose, and rebuked the wind, and said unto the sea, Peace, be still. And the wind ceased, and there was a great calm" (Mark 4:39).

"Peace, be still" is all Jesus had to say, and the wind and waves stopped. This is the same thing we need to do when the nights become overwhelming and sleep eludes us. State confidently: "Peace, be still."

However you say it, make sure you speak the words aloud. Just allowing them to cross your mind isn't good enough. Thoughts are fleeting, but words are definite, concrete, and these words, spoken as a prayer to God, can allow you to switch the gears in your brain to a much slower gear. One that isn't filled with life and its troubles but one that praises God.

Now that we've switched gears, we can begin to meditate on God's Word. Focusing and concentrating on a short Bible verse or even a song or hymn can keep our focus on God, causing us to relax and rest.

So, when the nights seem long and your brain is running nonstop, find peace to still the anxiety and shift your focus to Christ.

Dear Lord, I cry out to You now, asking that You will give my mind peace and still my racing thoughts. I lay my anxiety, worry and concerns for tomorrow at Your feet. Help me to focus on Your words so that I am able to relax and rest. Be with me as I sleep, and give my mind the calm it needs so that I may refresh both my mind and body so I can do Your will tomorrow. In Jesus' Name, Amen.

FOR THE TIMES I JUST CAN'T
Janelle Reinbold

"Come to me, all who labor and are heavy laden, and I will give you rest. Take my yoke upon you, and learn from me, for I am gentle and lowly in heart, and you will find rest for your souls. For my yoke is easy, and my burden is light." **Matthew 11:28-30 (ESV)**

"Can't is just an excuse not to try." True. At least most of the time ...

Just a glance down at the limp sling hanging awkwardly at my right side, with stiff fingers peeking out, is a reminder of the many times this past week when I have found myself having no rational and reasonable words to say except "I can't."

I don't like this helpless feeling. Not being able to take care of even the simplest of daily responsibilities creates anxiety. The kind of anxiety that keeps me up at night, fretting and stressing over how in the world each task someone was counting on me to complete is going to get done.

Although most of us work hard to resist feeling helpless, we all run into different types of daily stressors that seem to fall into the dreaded "I legitimately can't" category. Like when something we have no control over is an obstacle to meeting a need. Or when someone is stubbornly in our way. Sometimes, unhealed emotional wounds hold us back while physical limitations can force us to move ahead into situations we don't feel comfortable with. This whole "can't" thing can feel heavy, can't it?

Which is why I've been finding great comfort in Jesus' words found in Matthew 11:28-30, where He invites all of us who find ourselves weary and carrying heavy burdens to come to Him. Because He is gentle and humble in heart, we can find rest by learning from Him. And while carrying out our daily tasks, we can take His light and easy yoke upon ourselves. What an invitation!

Lately, I've been noticing an interesting way that God comes through and does lighten our heavy burdens: He often seems to make up the difference for our limitations by carrying things we legitimately can't.

This is much like what happens when a younger ox is yoked to an older, more skilled one for training purposes. While the younger is learning, the older makes up for the various ways his weaker apprentice is limited. What an accurate picture of what is actually happening when Jesus and I are walking through life together. He, who is clearly the stronger and more skilled of the two of us, carries what I can't. And in the process, I'm learning from Him.

Sometimes, Jesus carries what we can't by making problems disappear. Other times, He reveals solutions we never could have thought of on our own. Or provides the people and resources we need. He can even change our perspective on either what really matters in our situation or the timing in which things need to get done. And there are even times He can give us miraculous strength, courage and creativity to do things we can't do.

I never know how Jesus is going to help me until I cry out to Him, take up His yoke, and stop striving and straining to control things to make them work in the ways I think they should.

Jesus, thank You for understanding my human reality that I do have legitimate limitations. You are so good, loving and kind against the backdrop of irritations, stresses and even the very worst life can throw at me. I can rest my head knowing not only that You can carry what I can't tomorrow but that You love to do so. In Jesus' Name, Amen.

WALKING IN JESUS' UNFORCED RHYTHMS OF GRACE
Christina Marie Post

"Give all your worries and cares to God, for he cares about you."
1 Peter 5:7 (NLT)

Have you ever felt alone ... weary ... burdened ... even hopeless at times? Have you felt that ache in your soul for rest? The feeling that true, soul-deep peace seems just beyond reach. The concern that life keeps asking more of you than you have to offer. Maybe you've experienced that bone-deep tiredness that wears your emotions thin. And then there are the thoughts and worries that swirl in your head in the dark of night when you wish you could be sleeping.

In the midst of all of this, right there in the middle of real life, the Savior waits. He is ever present. Always ready. Whispering. Waiting. Gently calling, *Come away, My beloved. Come away with Me. Let Me teach you. Let Me whisper My Truth deep in your heart. Let Me show you how I see you. Let Me calm you with My love.*

But then there they are again ... the clamoring thoughts, the climbing anxiety, the chorus of voices in our heads, saying, *But what about this? Remember that? Don't forget this other thing.* And off we go into the endless distractions that call for our attention but offer nothing but exhaustion and depletion in exchange.

Yet the truth remains: We have a good Shepherd who delights in renewing our strength, and spending time in His presence can bring refreshment to our weary souls. I've been caught in the trap of believing that, unless I can get away for focused time with the Lord, I can't really find the nourishing refreshment my soul so desperately longs for. However, the truth is that Jesus is right by my side 24/7, and He offers me rest in the midst of my real life.

So, my friend, when we lay our heads on the pillows at night, and our thoughts begin to swirl, let's turn our attention to our Savior and release our cares and concerns to Him. One way I've learned to do this is by specifically naming things on my mind and releasing them to the Lord in prayer.

The invitation of 1 Peter 5:7 — *"Give all your worries and cares to God, for he cares about you"* — carries imagery, in the original Greek language, of shifting a heavy burden from your shoulders and flinging it upon another. Jesus Himself offers to carry our burdens for us. We can release them to Him and entrust every circumstance and situation fully into His capable hands.

As we respond to this invitation from Jesus, the heavy weight of responsibility and desire to control the outcome melts away as we grow in trusting the Lord. Psalm 27:13 encourages us: "*Yet I am confident I will see the* Lord's *goodness while I am here in the land of the living* (NLT).

The Lord is good! Together let's learn to walk in the unforced rhythms of grace Jesus offers us and experience soul-deep rest as we trust in the goodness of the Lord.

Dear Jesus, thank You for inviting me to entrust my heavy burdens to You. I praise You for being trustworthy and faithful. Please show me more of how You see me. Help me to understand afresh Your beautiful and rich love for me. Thank You for calling me to Yourself and making me Your friend. Now as I share the burdens of my heart with You, naming them specifically, I choose to release them to You, knowing that You are good, capable and loving. Please remind me of Your Truth and help me to rest in Your tender, loving care for me tonight. In Jesus' Name, Amen.

FIVE MORE MINUTES
Holly Murray

"Be still and know that I am God; I will be exalted among the nations, I will be exalted in the earth." **Psalm 46:10 (MEV)**

"Get some rest. Your eyes look like you've been working too hard," said the comment on my social media post.

That wasn't the message I intended with the selfie I posted, but I thought about the week's schedule. Each day brought news of an obligation only I could fill.

"I don't mind!"

"Sure, I have time."

"I can do that."

"I'd be happy to help!"

One by one, my heartfelt responses shrank my calendar's capacity.

The click of the keyboard and scratch of the pen become constant companions. Groceries ordered, a meal hastily thrown together, one last email answered with another swig of coffee as I check one more box on the list.

"I don't know how you do it," people tell me. This well-intentioned but unhealthy food for the weary soul feeds my pride and pushes me to the next scheduled task. Before I realize it, the sun has set and my excuse — "Almost done! Just five more minutes!" — escapes my lips again.

In this multi-tasking, work-from-anywhere, high-speed society, taking time to be still seems fruitless. Our hearts swell with accolades for the productivity and skill we bring to the table, but then we wince when we realize we've missed another morning with Jesus. We couldn't spare five minutes.

How often do we choose to be still — to sit, read the Word of God and listen for His voice? Our Father calls to us, *"Be still and know that I am God"* (Psalm 46:10). Be still! Cease, relax, withdraw and let go. Sounds heavenly, doesn't it?

The antidote for exhaustion from our overextended calendars isn't just being still, however, or He would have stopped with that command. We are to know that He is God. He is the Creator of the world, the One who cannot fail, who loves us without measure and whose promises are trustworthy.

He desires for us to *know* Him and wants a relationship with us. He already knows every part of us, but His longing is for us to know *Him*.

Part of intimacy is the privacy in which secrets are whispered between two. God wants this kind of intimacy with us. He longs to tell us private things meant just for us. He wants us to really know Him and experience who He is and His great love for us. He wants us to know we are worth all the time He spends pursuing us, no matter how many times we push His relentlessness to the side with promises of "Just give me five more minutes. I'm almost done."

What can you do in five minutes? There are lists of small tasks you can accomplish in that amount of time. But the real question is: What can He do with your five minutes?

Take five minutes and be still with Him today. Open His Word. Let Him whisper the secret joys He has in store for you. Allow Him to ease every tension and bring you the true rest your soul needs. Relax, and know Him. These will be the best-spent minutes of your day.

Father, thank You for Your relentless pursuit, and love for me. Today I choose to cease striving for perfection and let go of self-reliance. I recognize the true gift of time with You and will be intentional about spending my day with You. Forgive me for taking time with You for granted and for being more concerned about people-pleasing and self-promotion than pleasing and trusting You. Today, as I meditate on the truths of Your Word, I will listen for Your whisper. You created work and rest, and I trust You to help me plan my day to make the most of each. In Jesus' Name, Amen.

REACHING A BREAKING POINT
Jamie Heath

"But we have this treasure in jars of clay to show that this all-surpassing power is from God and not from us."
2 Corinthians 4:7 (NIV)

I want to quit. Give up.

I stand in front of my class with a smile on my face, but I'm crying on the inside. I ask myself, *Why am I here?*

Teaching at a public high school during a pandemic brings an exponentially higher amount of stress than I have ever faced in my career.

Breaking up a fight in the hallway, consoling a girl who is having a difficult time with some "mean girls," writing last-minute letters of recommendation, finding time to use the restroom — these are regular day-to-day events of a high school teacher. Add in the typical work demands such as emails, phone calls, meetings, presentations, reports, deadlines and the extra chaos of what COVID-19 brings. These don't even include all the lesson planning and teaching, which is the heart of my job. Day after day, this becomes exhausting and leads to burnout.

Many of us have experienced stressful times in our careers — whether we are stay-at-home moms with little ones all day, CEOs of major corporations or clerks at the grocery store. We've all had those "breaking point" moments when we want to walk away and quit.

This key verse reminds us that, in these stressful times, we are God's precious vessels who can be used to bring glory to Him: *"But we have this treasure in jars of clay to show that this all-surpassing power is from God and not from us"* (2 Corinthians 4:7).

The Apostle Paul was speaking about the struggle he and his co-workers were suffering as they spread the Truth of the gospel. They were feeling defeated and broken. Paul drew this comparison that humans are like jars made of clay where God keeps His treasure. The treasure is the light of God that can shine in all the darkness. We are like jars of clay that can easily break or crack. But as a jar of clay would begin to crack under pressure, this would then reveal the light hidden inside: our faith in God.

We feel broken, but our suffering is minimal compared to Jesus' suffering on the cross. Our suffering here on earth is short compared to eternity with Him. We should not quit; though God does not call us to remain in suffering for suffering's sake, we should not walk away from what God is calling us to do for His sake. We should keep going. Our strength and determination show others that God is omnipotent and He gives us the power to survive. God uses us to exemplify perseverance to bring glory to Him.

The next time I'm standing in front of my class, asking myself, *Why am I here?*, I will remember that God allows me to let the light of the gospel shine through me. My faith in Him brings me peace and calm, knowing He is in control and I am not.

Dear heavenly Father, please forgive me for wanting to surrender under challenging times instead of being the vessel to bring You glory. Please keep reminding me to live my life to magnify Your name and not myself. Remind me that my suffering is small compared to Your suffering on the cross and that one day I will spend eternity with You in all Your glory. In Jesus' Name, Amen.

FROM BITTER TO BLESSED
Julie Clark

"O Israel, the one who formed you says, 'Do not be afraid, for I have ransomed you. I have called you by name; you are mine.'"
Isaiah 43:1b (NLT)

The names we call ourselves reveal much about how we see ourselves.

Where I live in Africa, receiving a new name is an honor. Upon meeting a foreigner and developing a friendship, the local people will bestow their family name upon the visitor as a demonstration of hospitality and welcome. The stranger becomes "part of the family." This "you are one of us now" gesture indicates complete acceptance and evokes a comforting sense of belonging.

It's even more comforting to know that God knows us each by name. The prophet Isaiah recorded this message from God to His chosen people: "*I have called you by name; you are mine*" (Isaiah 43:1b).

But what happens when we change our name or identity? Does God still know us? Do we still belong? What happens when we fail to see ourselves through God's eyes and we take on a persona that is not meant to be ours?

In the story of Ruth, Naomi attempted to do this. Her given name means "pleasant." But after suffering the tragedy of losing her husband and both of her sons while living in a foreign land, Naomi could no longer call herself "pleasant." This grieving widow was now left alone, without a male family member to protect or provide for her. She determined to return to her homeland, to Bethlehem, accompanied by her daughter-in-law Ruth.

Upon arrival, Naomi bluntly admonished everyone: "'*Don't call me Naomi,*' she told them. '*Call me Mara, because the Almighty has made my life very bitter. I went away full but the* Lord *has brought me back empty*'" (Ruth 1:20-21a, NIV). In her grief and disappointment, Naomi changed her name from "pleasant" to "bitter." She now wanted to be identified only by her misfortune. And she blamed God. But God was not angry with her. Instead, He had a wonderful blessing planned for her.

Naomi's daughter-in-law Ruth met and married Boaz, Naomi's kinsman.

Ruth gave birth to Obed, a son, making Naomi a grandmother and reestablishing her family line. This birth placed Naomi in the genealogy that led to King David and later to Jesus Himself. (Ruth 4:17) From the abandoned, despairing, childless widow springs forth the King of kings! She is honored, blessed and called Naomi once more.

Initially, Naomi saw her circumstances as too overwhelming to ever be any different than what they were. She believed she was invisible to God and there was no future for her, which led to hopelessness and bitterness. But Naomi did not have to remain bitter. Our loving God tenderly orchestrated a beautiful second chance for her, a future He had in mind for her all along.

God is waiting to hand out second chances. He knows you, and you are His! Sometimes we don't sense God near us because of a blockade of inaccurate identity we've given ourselves.

Maybe you've mislabeled yourself. Let God rename you! He can transform a negative self-image into something beautiful and new. He did this for Naomi. And He can for you, too.

God, my Father, thank You for loving me as You loved Naomi. I know that if You can make pleasant what is bitter, then You can turn despair into hope, fear into courage, rage into gentleness, worthlessness into treasure, and grief into joy. Show me how You see me. I ask You to take the negative, inaccurate label I've given myself and make me new. I give You permission to transform me. Tonight, I will rest peacefully, believing that tomorrow my perception of myself will begin to change. Thank You, Father, for what You will do in my life. In Jesus' Name, Amen.

THE WANDERERS, THE PRISONERS, THE FOOLS AND THE DISCOURAGED
Kara Niewenhuis

"Then they cried out to the Lᴏʀᴅ in their trouble, and he delivered them from their distress." **Psalm 107:6 (NIV)**

I lay my head on my pillow at night, and almost immediately the familiar sequence takes place: My breathing, which has been normal all day, seems shallower and a bit strained. I counteract it by taking a deep, slow breath, holding it in and releasing it. But still my lungs can't seem to reach their fill. Sometimes my thoughts dart around like mayhem. Other times I can't even locate the thought that makes me anxious. Always, the rest my body craves is interrupted by the unrest in my mind and spirit.

When did the anxiety begin? It was almost imperceptible ... somewhere in between a pregnancy, a pandemic and a move across the country.

Psalm 107 is a beautiful, aching poem that gives a graphic picture of four different groups of people, each suffering his or her own crisis. It's like four different verses of the same song, but the refrain is always the same, and (spoiler alert!) the Lord *always delivers.*

The Wanderers (verses 4-9) can't find a place to settle down; they are hungry and thirsty. When they cry out to God, He leads them straightaway to a city and satisfies their hunger and thirst.

The Prisoners (verses 10-16) are in darkness and gloom, in bondage because of their own rebellious choices. When they cry out to God, He breaks their iron chains. I imagine this happening in a roaring, Hulk-like liberation.

The Fools (verses 17-22) have made disobedient choices that have brought them affliction. They can't eat and are close to death. When they cry out to God, He heals with His Word and brings them back from death.

The Discouraged (verses 23-30) are going about their regular lives when storms hit them so violently that they can't even stand straight anymore. They lose all ability to reason or rescue themselves. When they cry out to God, *"He still[s] the storm to a whisper... and he guide[s] them to their desired haven"* (Psalm 107:29-30, NIV).

What keeps your body, mind and spirit from rest this evening? Is it the continuous hunger to be filled and settled, but the media, movies and food you consume always leave you feeling emptier than before? Is it that sin, that vice, that has wrapped you so tightly you feel you will never escape? Is it the constant replaying of every decision, every "I'm not enough," every failure from your day? Or is it the realization that life has hit you from every direction, battering you down until you're overwhelmed and discouraged?

Be encouraged. Just like the needy ones in our psalm, we can cry out to our Savior. *"Then they cried out to the Lord in their trouble, and he delivered them from their distress."* (Psalm 107:6) He is holy and mighty and perfect. With every cry comes deliverance.

Lord, You are my strong and mighty Deliverer. When I'm lost, stuck, foolish or simply discouraged, Your promise to me is the same. You are the God who saves. I cry out to You tonight and believe that You can and You will deliver me from my distress. Calm my body and my mind and my spirit. I breathe in You and release all anxiety. Let me rest safely and peacefully under Your care. I claim Your promises and claim Your victory. "In peace I will lie down and sleep, for you alone, Lord, make me dwell in safety." (Psalm 4:8, NIV)

family concerns

PRAYERS AND DEVOTIONS FOR SLE

A WORLD OF WORRY

clear mind,

peaceful

heart

GRACE AND REST FOR THE LONE PARENT
Shovorne Adams

"Don't be anxious about anything; rather, bring up all of your requests to God in your prayers and petitions, along with giving thanks. Then the peace of God that exceeds all understanding will keep your hearts and minds safe in Christ Jesus."
Philippians 4:6-7 (CEB)

I slowed my pace to match the speed of the heavy rotating doors and returned good-morning smiles and nods to my colleagues. As my heels clip-clopped through the bright reception area, I gave myself a once-over in the reflection of the floor-to-ceiling office windows. I looked professional as always. So did my practiced smile.

It was effortless to turn on perfectionism at work. The rules for performing at work came easily. Why isn't there a switch to turn on perfect parenting? Where is the single-motherhood rulebook? I logged on and waited for the usual flurry of emails to update in my inbox but couldn't log off from thoughts of home. How could I protect my sons, keep them safe from the snares and pitfalls of secondary school and the bullies? My two boys are my everything. I mentally scanned through a list of people I could ask for help. The list was short. I sighed as the downs of lone parenting attempted to sabotage the ups.

Lunchtime came, and I rushed down the corridor to a meeting room, where once a week a small group of believers met. In a corporate building with thousands of people, God certainly played a hand in connecting me with Christians for such a time as this. I had no more tears left to cry, but I had more room for the prayers of the saints. No one to step in physically, but these were the folks who would lean in spiritually. Prayer. It's the only solid answer I had. Putting my children's needs at the altar.

It was my turn to share my prayer request next. "Can we pray for my two boys, please?" I explained the troubling scenarios at school, and on bended knees, we bowed our heads and spoke with our heavenly Father.

Feeling lighter, I lifted my head from my clipboard as I walked down the corridor later that afternoon. Peter, the leader of our workplace prayer group, headed toward me. I looked through his gold-rimmed spectacles, examining his wise eyes. "I want to tell you that God cares about your boys, and they'll be OK, but God also cares about you. He watches over them, and He also has you in His arms."

I responded with silence. His message was so simple yet so profound. I'd heard of God's love for me, but I needed that reminder that day. I was trying to hold it all together for my children, but God just wanted to hold me. When I carried my worries and struggled to let them go, God wanted to carry me — if I would let Him.

There are no parents with all the answers. As a parent, you show up with your best, and even when you're not feeling at your best, God does the rest. His grace is sufficient for you. Rest in it. With God, you're never on your own.

My forever-faithful Father, I bring my children's needs before You and ask that You give me the grace to love on them from a place of abundance as You fill my cup. Though I don't have all the answers to the challenges they'll face in the world, may they have the wisdom of Your Word to help them navigate this life. Thank You for how You carry me, hold me and love me, reminding me that I am never alone on this journey. You are the everlasting God, the beginning and the end and all that is in between. The worries that have become heavy I hand over to You as my hope rests in the assurance of Your promises of peace and love. May Your rhythms of grace be the binding thread throughout our home. As I lead my children, lead me beside the still and peaceful waters. In Jesus' Name, Amen.

PRAYING THE PROMISE OF PRESENCE OVER WORRY
Amy Morgan

"Have I not commanded you? Be strong and courageous. Do not be frightened, and do not be dismayed, for the LORD your God is with you wherever you go." Joshua 1:9 (ESV)

I adore listening to the prayers of young children. They are so sweet and pure. There is no pretense. Children pray how they feel and aren't concerned about saying the right words.

When my boys were small, I cherished our times of praying together. It made my heart melt hearing their sweet little voices thanking God for blessings and praying for family and friends. However, in the midst of these prayers, I began to notice a theme of worry emerge. My son prayed every day that God would be with us and keep us safe. Over and over, he'd pray for safety — for himself, friends and family.

Ironically, I began to worry that he was worried about safety and wondered where this worry was coming from. I was tangled in worry about the worry trap.

This worry tangle is a very perplexing place we often find ourselves in — worried about worry, until we bring it to the Lord. As I sought the Lord and a trusted friend, the worry trap began untangling. My son's prayers were mirroring mine. I was praying daily for protection over my children, asking God to "be with them" whenever they left my presence. Then while they were gone, I worried more and prayed over and over for God's presence until they returned to me.

God knows we will worry and be afraid. In Joshua 1:9, God says, *"Have I not commanded you? Be strong and courageous. Do not be frightened, and do not be dismayed, for the LORD your God is with you wherever you go."*

The Lord is clear. When He says, *"Have I not commanded you?"* God reminds Joshua that He has told him this before. (Deuteronomy 31:8) Plus, God was faithful to be with Joshua then, and He means it now. Joshua needed to trust God's promise.

Jesus reiterates this promise to be near us in Matthew 28:20b, saying, *"And behold, I am with you always, to the end of the age"* (ESV).

Joshua did not need to be frightened or dismayed. I do not need to be frightened or dismayed.

You do not need to be frightened or dismayed, for the Lord our God is with us wherever we go. My prayers for God to be with my children were prayers of worry. But God calls us to freedom from worry, promising He is with us wherever we go. We don't need to ask for it. It is a gift we receive.

So I changed my prayers over my children. I began praying, *Thank You, Lord, that You are with us wherever we go.* As I prayed these words over and over, they changed me. I began to believe they were true. I began to trust them. And as my prayers changed, my children's prayers shifted from prayers of worry to confidence in God's promise.

I'm truly thankful that God is with us wherever we go. What a gift! Believing and praying this promise over ourselves and others defeats worry with truth and trust.

Now, when I feel worry creeping in, I thank God that He is with me, my children, my family and my friends no matter where we go.

Dear heavenly Father, thank You for being with us wherever we go. There is no place we can go to escape Your presence. Help me to trust this promise. When worry creeps in, when I am alone or separated from loved ones, remind me of Your presence in my life and theirs. Thank You for Your promise of presence; may I take refuge in it. In Jesus' Name, Amen.

GATHERING GRACE TO TRY AGAIN
Susan Davidson

"And when they had eaten their fill, he told his disciples, 'Gather up the leftover fragments, that nothing may be lost.'"
John 6:12 (ESV)

I lost my temper with my husband, failing once again to keep my emotions under control. I was making progress, but now I was back to the drawing board again. The enemy was quick to knock on my door, and this time he had brought his cohorts named *Worry* and *Failure* along for the visit. I am not proud to acknowledge that I invited them in.

By afternoon, I had allowed them to convince me I would never be the strong Christian lady I desired to be. I was also now confident that I was the worst wife imaginable.

I finally gathered enough strength to pray. I had decided maybe it was time to pour my heart out to God instead of fretting to myself. Surprisingly, my mood began to shift as I reached for my Bible to allow God to join the conversation.

As I was reading about the miracle of Jesus and the feeding of the multitude, a verse I had barely noticed before seemed to lift off the page and grab my heart. John 6:12 reads, *"And when they had eaten their fill, he told his disciples, 'Gather up the leftover fragments, that nothing may be lost.'"*

Jesus had miraculously given them provision and took special care that even the smallest portion that was left had a purpose. No piece was wasted that day because we serve a Savior who takes extraordinary care with even fragments and leftovers. He especially cares about the broken pieces of our lives.

We can be so quick to throw in the towel when we fall short of our expectations. We can easily forget that God doesn't run out of grace in our moments of weakness and never gives up on us. Momentary shortcomings can never alter or diminish the love of our devoted heavenly Father.

The wondrous thing is that God carefully crafts every piece of our story. He even uses our broken pieces and failures to showcase His grace and redemption. Not one crumb of our miraculous story is lost or thrown away.

Over the years, I've learned that God can turn anything around for our good, but our enemy's purpose is to steal, kill and destroy us. (John 10:10) He shows no mercy and delights in pushing us down on our worst days. He loves to entice us to make mistakes and then endeavors to persuade us we will never amount to anything for God because of them. He wants us to waste our lives worrying over what was rather than embracing God's grace for what can be.

I wish I could tell you that I have never lost my temper with my husband since that day 36 years ago, but I can tell you I am no longer as apt to throw in the towel. I have learned that even when I fall short, I can gather up what remains, grab hold of Jesus and try again. Because of His grace, nothing is completely lost, despite what the enemy will tell you.

Dear heavenly Father, thank You for Your all-sufficient grace and mercy. Whenever I fall short, You give me the strength to gather up what remains and try again. I never have to worry that You have given up on me. You always meet me wherever I am, especially when I struggle to have faith to believe I can be who You say I can be. Thank You for giving me provision to meet all my needs and for forever helping me grow into the Christian woman and wife You have called me to be. In Jesus' Name, Amen.

FAITH FOR THE FEEDER
Erin Nestico

"But let him ask in faith, with no doubting, for the one who doubts is like a wave of the sea that is driven and tossed by the wind."
James 1:6 (ESV)

The bitter wind stung my eyes as I lugged the unwieldy tote of birdseed through the snow toward our bird feeders. Six months ago, bird conservationists asked that we refrain from feeding the birds because a contagious eye disease was spreading as the birds assembled at communal feeders. But with winter's arrival, the advisory and its precautions were lifted.

As I struggled to fill the feeder with my thick-gloved hands, I wondered if the birds would come before nightfall. So many months had passed with no provisions; would they doubt this house had anything to offer them? With unanswered questions swirling through my mind, I finished up, placed the tote in the garage and headed inside.

As I puttered around my kitchen a few hours later, I noticed birds by the feeder.

I cried out "yay" and ran to the dining room window to get a better look. Chickadees, blue jays, woodpeckers, juncos and cardinals all feasted on the suet, sunflower seeds and cracked corn.

They had a need; I met that need, and they responded swiftly. I pondered the birds' unwavering trust and was pleased with how they came in faith. It was then God spoke to my heart, saying, *You have a need. I want to meet that need. I offer you peace of mind and wisdom, but you need to trust and come to Me in faith as readily as the birds.*

As my children get older, my worries for them grow. The current list includes college choices, dating partners and driving. Am I giving the best guidance and making the wisest parenting decisions?

When we ask for wisdom, James 1:6 instructs us to *"ask in faith, with no doubting, for the one who doubts is like a wave of the sea that is driven and tossed by the wind."*

I have a choice when it comes to guiding my children into adulthood.

I can toss and turn during sleepless nights and wonder if I'm making the right decisions, or I can come to God's storehouse of love, peace and wisdom. Proverbs 2:7 (ESV) tells us, "*he stores up sound wisdom for the upright ...*" and Psalm 107:9 (NLT) states, "*he satisfies the thirsty and fills the hungry with good things.*"

Whether it's wisdom, love or peace, God has a tote overflowing with whatever I need. There are no advisories that can make Him withhold His provisions. Instead, He waits for me to come and feast. His heart fills with joy when He knows I'm ready to receive His offerings. And I imagine He shouts joyfully when I trust Him to guide me through the tough parenting years as effortlessly as the birds trust me to get them through the long, frigid winter.

As I lie down in bed each night, in faith, I pray for God to give me the wisdom I need in the months and years ahead. I hunger and thirst for His guidance. Then, without any doubts, I'm ready to partake of God's offerings and get a good night's sleep.

Dear Lord, thank You for providing me with the wisdom I need in my parenting decisions. I accept Your love and peace as I lie down to sleep, knowing You are able and ready to fulfill all my needs. In Jesus' Name, Amen.

HOLDING TIGHT TO TRUST
Heather Hutchinson

"Love ... always protects, always trusts, always hopes, always perseveres. Love never fails." **1 Corinthians 13:6-8a (NIV)**

After slipping off my sneakers, I followed the technician into the exam room, where he centered my body under the monstrous X-ray machine before stepping away. "Exhale. Now, hold," he spoke in a muffled voice through the window in the adjoining room. Then, after he snapped the shot: "OK, relax."

For over a decade, I experienced inflammation and hip pain due to bone spurs and deteriorated cartilage, and the X-rays confirmed that my 40-year-young hip joint was bone on bone.

Unfortunately, my hip wasn't the only thing suffering in my life. My marriage was struggling too, and many times I wished I had an emotional detector to pinpoint the trigger that caused the brokenness in our relationship the way the X-ray conveyed the cause of my chronic pain.

Eventually, I came to see that just as my tight muscles and arthritic femur often prevented me from being able to sit, bend or carry out my daily activities, the recurring rude assumptions and defensive reactions to my husband's innocent behavior resulted in conflict, frustration and the deterioration of our friendship.

My distrust was causing injury.

My distrust was causing more pain.

My distrust was causing the hurt in our marriage to continue.

My heart ached to love and trust my husband fearlessly just as I longed to feel the stride of my legs stretching further into a sprint.

But instead, I limped. I'd limped most of my life, holding tight to a crutch of distrust and expecting it to hold me up.

In time, I realized that in order to move forward in my marriage, I would need to exchange the distrustful thoughts rooted in a fear of rejection for the stable truth of God's unfailing Word: *"Love trusts."* First Corinthians 13:6-8a says, *"Love ... always protects, always trusts, always hopes, always perseveres. Love never fails."*

Trust is defined as "to believe in or to have a belief in the reliability, truth, ability or strength of someone or something." God's Word, the source of all truth and wisdom, declares that the never-failing love of Christ's work on the cross can be trusted. It declares that we can confidently stand on and peacefully rest in the faithfulness of God to help heal our hearts and our relationships. I've found God's Word to be true, and as my trust in God has grown, I'm increasingly able to trust my husband too.

Even though we get triggered and sometimes limp, we can always limp to Jesus. He promises to pick us up and, much like an X-ray, will shine the light of His Word into every worrisome thought instigated by past hurt. His voice will whisper into our hearts, "I will never leave you or forsake you." As we begin to believe what Jesus has said about who He is and who we are in Him, the Holy Spirit will transform our troubled minds and empower us to love as He loves us.

Dear Jesus, help me to continually trust in Your love for me, and help me to lay my life down daily in Your arms. Lord, I'm often afraid of being hurt again, and You know how all the "what ifs" play over in my mind. But I know fear is not from You. You have not given me a spirit of fear but one of power, love and self-discipline. Lord, please take my worries and help me replace them with Your unfailing Truth. Thank You that Your perfect love casts out all fear and that Your love never fails. In Jesus' Name, Amen.

WHEN CARELESS THOUGHTS CREATE SLEEPLESS NIGHTS
Mary Folkerts

"You keep him in perfect peace whose mind is stayed on you, because he trusts in you." Isaiah 26:3 (ESV)

The sunny days of August were quickly drawing to a close, and I could feel anxiety biting at my heels. Fall, with its golden light, brilliant colors and farm harvests, had always been a favorite time for me until recently. Now it brought anxiety, a feeling so intense it left me afraid for summer's end.

We raise our children to leave us one day and be independent, but for me, when September arrived and they headed back to university, I experienced feelings of profound loss. The seasons in my life were changing, and I had to choose how I would face it. My choice would be the framework for the thoughts I entertained. I could mourn the silence at the dinner table, or I could turn the page to a new chapter and embrace the future. I chose the mourning, and my thoughts slipped into a spiraling rut of despair.

These despairing thoughts wreaked havoc with my mind, causing visceral reactions in my body. I began to experience panic attacks, racing thoughts, feelings of hopelessness, inability to focus on tasks, bouts of tears and restless nights.

The thoughts we entertain in our waking hours are the ones that will keep us tossing and turning at night. Isaiah 26:3 gives us detailed instructions on finding the peace we desperately seek: *"You keep him in perfect peace whose mind is stayed on you, because he trusts in you"* (emphasis added).

This verse calls us to "stay our mind" or lean hard into Jesus — with good reason. The battle for our minds is a war we must fight with complete dependence on Christ. Our emotions can confuse the facts, making them unreliable. For example, my emotions told me that my job as a mom was coming to an end; God's Truth said that I was only transitioning in my role, and I needed to keep looking ahead to new and exciting adventures. Staying my mind on Jesus illuminated my path with Truth, breaking the power of the lies that had me bound in despair.

We must harness our thought life with military precision. Have you ever stared at a particular object so intensely that everything in your peripheral view is blurred? That is how we need to focus on Christ. Not with a passing glance at the beginning of the day but with determined resolve that all of our thoughts filter through our gaze directed at Jesus.

Is your thought true? If not, divert your mind back to Truth. Is your thought honorable, just and pure? If not, divert your mind back to what you know to be pure. Is your thought lovely and excellent? If your answer is no, divert your mind back to the beauty of Christ. (Philippians 4:8) Too often, we assume we are helpless to change our thinking and allow our minds to meander in the minefields.

Meandering thoughts produce worry, and worry during the day creates unrest at night. Fixing our minds on Jesus, trusting Him to provide, will bring peace no matter the circumstance.

Dear Lord, I lie down in peace. I close my eyes, resting assured You never sleep and are ever watchful over me. Help me release my worries and lay them at Your feet. You hold my children, even when I cannot, in a tender embrace; they are surrounded by Your fierce love. I slow my breath, allowing You to take my imagination and paint peace in extravagant strokes. Sweep away my anxious thoughts. Replace them with the image of You, Jesus, standing guard while I sleep in peace. In Jesus' Name, Amen.

WHAT I HEARD
Jean Pfeifer

"Hearing this, Jesus said to Jairus, 'Don't be afraid; just believe, and she will be healed.'" **Luke 8:50 (NIV)**

Relief! She's home.

No, wait. Something's wrong!

She's a mess. Disheveled. Defiant.

A brief pit stop to freshen up and she's gone again.

My teenage daughter is home for the summer from college in another city — kind of. She's been in and out for days and nights. Where is she? What is she doing? Who is she with?

Slowly small clues emerge. Her college boyfriend has followed her home. Things aren't good between the two of them, but we can't talk about it. I'm resigned to wait until she reappears.

You'd think after 10 years of experience I would have mastered single parenting and would know what to do. Mastered? No. Experienced? Yes. I've had lots of experience, both talking and listening — sometimes to her, many times to Jesus. Lacking wisdom to be a single parent, I've cried out to God often, *"Show me your ways, Lord, teach me your paths"* (Psalm 25:4, NIV). And He did, training me through His Word and by His Spirit, every day. As I learned, a clear pattern unfolded: life's storms, my cries, His voice, my trust, His peace.

That's why I'm kneeling now beside my bed in the middle of the night, face wet, cries desperate. I'm calling to the Master of storms who commands winds and waves to be still.

And then it happens.

Two words are spoken quietly into my troubled mind: *Jairus' daughter.*

I get up and read the story in the Bible about Jairus, who pleaded at the feet of Jesus for the Savior to come home with him and heal his dying daughter. On the way to Jairus' home, news came that she was dead.

"Hearing this, Jesus said to Jairus, 'Don't be afraid; just believe, and she will be healed.'" (Luke 8:50)

And she was. Healed. Brought back to life. By Jesus.

As I read the story, Jesus speaks those same words to me. I listen. I believe. I trust His promise. I'm not sure what to pray, but it's OK. It isn't *what I'm praying* that settles my heart. It is *what I'm hearing* — from Jesus.

Years before, my young daughter worried incessantly that I would leave like her daddy did. When she was apart from me, she phoned often. She needed to hear my voice to calm her worries. Now I need that too. I need to hear Jesus' voice. When I do, I willfully trust Him, and He gives me peace.

Jesus has an uncanny, lovely way of settling worried parents and helping them sleep. The sound of His voice, the authority and comfort of His message, calm my heart, as they have on countless other nights when I've gotten up and read Scripture. I might not wake up to "sunshine, lollipops and rainbows" the next day, but I'll wake up to a promise from God that I can cling to, and eventually Jesus will bring her home.

Experience has taught me that peace guards my heart day and night when I hear from Jesus and trust what I hear.

Jesus, You slept in a boat during a dangerous storm. When the terrified disciples woke You up, the authority of Your words brought calm. You're amazing! Speak Your words over the worry that holds me captive. Help me to trust what I hear so Your peace will bless me with sleep. As I read Scripture with You each day, please prepare me for nights like this by giving me Your promises. In Jesus' Name, Amen.

BEING FULL OF PEACE WHEN OUR NESTS ARE EMPTY
Terri Prahl

*"The L*ORD *will keep your going out and your coming in from this time forth and forevermore."* **Psalm 121:8 (ESV)**

Tossing and turning has become a reoccurring problem as I enter the empty-nest stage of my mothering journey. One of the greatest parenting challenges I have faced is learning to sleep peacefully after releasing my adult children to manage their own lives.

My days always came to a calming end when I knew my children were safely tucked in their beds under the perceived safety of their parents.

I think back to when they were small children and how they easily slipped into blissful slumber, fully expecting us to meet their every need. Watching them sleep without a care in the world brought peace to my own soul.

Even though my children were completely dependent for many of those years, they didn't seem to fret over their lack of control. Their ability to sleep in peace spoke of the trust they had in us.

I think about my life now — one child married and one living at home but gone more often than not. Sometimes our young adult daughter works late, hangs with friends or is out studying past my bedtime, and it's hard for me to lie down to sleep until I hear the garage door lifting, signaling her return.

The "what ifs" of worry are insidiously destructive if we allow them into our minds — especially right before our thoughts need to be slowing down for rest.

The truth is that my sense of control was an illusion. I could pay attention and care for my kids to the best of my ability, but I couldn't shield them from all the hard realities of life. Only God can protect them.

This bittersweet season is a reminder of who they belong to — who they belonged to all along.

In a time of fear and looming danger, as the Israelites journeyed long distances to Jerusalem to celebrate the feasts, Psalm 121:8 was sung, assuring them with these words: *"The LORD will keep your going out and your coming in from this time forth and forevermore."*

When my eyes can't see my adult children, I can rest assured that God never takes His eyes off those He loves. Wherever my children are — whatever good or bad decisions they make — God is watching over them according to His Word.

How can I sleep when I don't know where they are and can't see if they are safe?

- I remember that they belong to a God who keeps better tabs on them than I ever could.
- I rehearse the truth of Psalm 121 until I believe it.
- I remember that every word of Scripture that is true for me is equally true for my kids, no matter their age.

I can sleep because God never does. His eyes never close in slumber, nor does He lose track of any of His sheep.

Just as when my children were dependent yet fully trusting in our care, so can I close my eyes, quiet my mind and rest in the care of my Father's provision and under His watchful eye.

Father, wherever my grown kids are tonight, I am thankful Your eyes see where mine do not. Help me to trust You with them so I can lie down and sleep in peace. In their coming and going, I know You are aware and capable of directing their lives as well as mine. Help me to trust You, God. Instead of drowning in the "what ifs," may I be found singing Truth into the dark nights as the psalmist did. Calm my heart and bring Your peace. In Jesus' Name, Amen.

I DON'T KNOW WHAT TO SAY, GOD
Gretchen Leech

"... the Spirit helps us in our weakness. We do not know what we ought to pray for, but the Spirit himself intercedes for us through wordless groans." **Romans 8:26 (NIV)**

It was the dark hours of the night, and the fear that surrounded me was keeping me awake. Earlier that day my husband and I had gotten the news that his cancer had returned, and all I could do was replay it over and over in my mind. As I obsessed about the battle we were facing, I was overwhelmed and frightened by the possibility that I might lose Doug to cancer.

As I lay in bed next to my husband, who was sleeping soundly, I realized my body would not rest, so I crept out into our silent house. My emotions were like a roller coaster. I was grieved about what our family was going through and angry that God allowed Doug to be sick once more. I was puzzled by God's ways.

I knew I needed to talk to God, but I had no idea what to say. Was I supposed to shout angry obscenities at Him, or was I supposed to sit and beg for my husband's life?

I sat quietly and just said Jesus' name over and over. Then in my moment of greatest need, He spoke to me on that cold, dark night. He told me to sing and to praise His name. I began singing Matt Maher's "Lord, I Need You":

"Lord, I come. I confess.
Bowing here, I find my rest.
Without You, I fall apart.
You're the One that guides my heart.
Lord, I need You, oh I need You.
Every hour, I need You.
My one defense, my righteousness,
Oh God, how I need You."

These words fell into my head like snowflakes falling onto a pond. My mind absorbed the words, and they streamed out of me straight to God. I did not need to shout or plead; I needed to rest in God's loving care. On that dark, lonely night, He was there with me.

I was reminded of a valuable lesson as I sat there frightened and lonely. In our times of despair and desperation, Jesus is always waiting for our call. It doesn't matter what we are going through — He will answer. He will fill us with promise and give us direction.

Romans 8:26 tells us, "*the Spirit himself intercedes for us through wordless groans.*" All we need to do is go to Jesus on bended knee, trusting Him.

That night, after singing softly and praising Him, I went back to bed and immediately fell asleep in His care.

I woke up the next morning ready to face whatever was coming our way because I knew our family was not alone. God was walking with us every step of the way, even carrying us when we were too weak to walk on our own. I knew our God would never forsake us.

Dear Lord, it is so hard to rest when the world is weighing heavy in my thoughts. When I'm at a loss, You are not; You know exactly what I need. Thank You for sending Your Spirit to intercede for me when I don't know what to pray. Clear my thoughts so I can focus on You instead of the despair around me. As I lay my head down, give me peace, rest and comfort. Give me the confidence that I will never be alone because You are always with me. You are always one step ahead of me with open arms, ready to catch me. Thank You for working in every situation, even when I'm blinded by my fear. In Jesus' Name, Amen.

trusting God during difficult times

PRAYERS AND DEVOTIONS FOR SLEEP IN A WORLD OF WORRY

clear mind,

peaceful

heart

HIS HEART WENT OUT TO HER
Elizabeth H. Patrick

"When the Lord saw her, his heart went out to her and he said, 'Don't cry.'" **Luke 7:13 (NIV)**

I curled up in my bedside chair, picking up my pen, journal and Bible, and thought half to myself and half to the Lord: *Here I am, again, about to journal the same prayer I've prayed for eight years.*

Not even sure I expected an answer anymore, I opened my Bible to Luke, where I'd been reading the past few days. I came to Chapter 7 and the story of the widow of Nain. I've read Luke many times, but the words from verse 13 captured my attention and settled something in my soul. I read them repeatedly. *"When the Lord saw her, his heart went out to her and he said, 'Don't cry.'"* (Luke 7:13)

With a large crowd of mourners in tow, this dear widow was on her way to bury her only son when she bumped into Jesus and a crowd of His followers at the city gate. After a command from Jesus, the dead man came back to life and began speaking.

Immediately prior to this miracle, Jesus came from Capernaum. Nain was approximately 30 miles uphill from Capernaum. It would have taken Jesus hours to walk there. Was it His plan all along to leave Capernaum at the hour He did and walk 30 miles so He would meet this grieving woman at just the right moment? Timing something so perfectly to meet someone at her most desperate place of need sounds just like something Jesus would do. Because individuals matter to Him.

I do want my circumstances to change, and I know He has the power to immediately change them like He did for the widow when He raised her son from the dead. But sitting there in my chair and reading the words Jesus spoke to her encouraged me so much. Jesus has the same attitude toward me because He's a very personal Savior. He looks at me. His heart goes out to me. And He is tender with my emotions, especially while I wait for answers to difficult prayers.

Whatever you're praying and waiting for — even if it's been eight long years — your Savior cares. Maybe you're crying out for a lost loved one, a broken marriage, a financial breakthrough, healing of an emotional wound, a mind free from anxiety and fear, a medical diagnosis or something else equally important. It's difficult to be patient when you've been praying for a long time — when there's seemingly no answer and an uncertain future lies ahead.

But even now, He is taking action to come to you — perfectly timed — because His heart goes out to you, and He will reach into your most needy places. And even if it's not with an immediate solution to your problem, it will be with compassion, comfort and peace.

Father, I know just as Your heart went out to the widow, it goes out to me. You see me. Right here. Right now. You're aware of my hopes, needs, dreams, desires, pain, hurts and losses. You're not just simply aware of me but You are taking action to come to my aid, and You time it perfectly. You have a gentle compassion for me and understand my emotions. You reach out Your hand to me, wipe my tears and encourage me with the tender words: "Don't cry." I may not understand, and sometimes it feels like my wait is unfairly long, but I trust You and ask You to strengthen me as I look to You for peace and rest while I wait. In Jesus' Name, Amen.

A HOLY "UGLY CRY"
Rachel Sims

"Arise, cry out in the night, as the watches of the night begin; pour out your heart like water in the presence of the Lord."
Lamentations 2:19a (NIV)

It was late Friday afternoon, and a storm was rolling in. Although I was tired of work, the thought of leaving the office and eating takeout on the couch alone, again, made my stomach twist into tiny knots.

I pushed the scary thought away, turned to my co-worker and made random conversation: "Maybe I'll play in the rain tonight. I did that all the time as a kid!"

She laughed and then said something I didn't expect: "You're going to be such a good mom."

The words hit a nerve in my soul, sending a shock down my spine and moisture to my eyes. The knots in my stomach tightened. I barely muttered, "Uh, thanks," as I grabbed my bag, shut down my computer and left the building, ignoring the 30 minutes left in my workday.

I sprinted to my car, sliding inside just as tears began sliding down my cheeks. I rested my head against the steering wheel and wept.

My sweet friend had no idea that she was bringing up one of my greatest fears. I was in a difficult season, and after years of unanswered prayers, I had convinced myself that I would never have a family of my own. These "ugly cries" were becoming more and more common.

You know the cries I'm talking about, right? The ones where you end up on the floor. The ones that require an entire box of Kleenex. The ones that arise from a mysterious place in your gut. The ones that make you wonder, *Where are You, God?*

During those years, God introduced me to a new kind of prayer. In biblical language, you'd call it a "lament." I like to call it a "holy 'ugly cry.'" Read how Lamentations 2:19a describes it:

"Arise, cry out in the night, as the watches of the night begin; pour out your heart like water in the presence of the Lord."

Lamentations is about a season of horrific suffering in Israel's history. Jerusalem had just been destroyed by the Babylonians, and this book records their honest prayers — full of grief, anger, bewilderment and doubt.

We have this big misunderstanding about prayer. Somehow, we've convinced ourselves that God is looking for polished prayers — bright, shiny and logical. But this verse paints a different picture. The Israelites were encouraged, even *commanded*, to simply come into God's presence and empty their hearts — no matter what was inside them.

Lament is the process of telling God what you are actually thinking, not what you think you should be thinking.

Friend, our God is so good. Psalm 34:18 (ESV) says that He is *"near to the brokenhearted."* He wants to be close to you when you're afraid and full of heartache. If you are weighed down by worries, don't wait until you have the "right" kind of prayer ready. Curl up in bed, grab some tissues and have a holy "ugly cry." Jesus will meet you there.

Father, sometimes I don't pray to You because I'm afraid to tell You what I'm really thinking. Please forgive me for excluding You from my heart. I accept Your invitation to come into Your presence and empty my heart. I know You're powerful enough to handle my questions and doubts and fears. Help me to fully understand what's inside of me so I can surrender it all to You. Thank You for being my friend, my comforter and my rescuer. In Jesus' Name, Amen.

LIKE DIRTY LAUNDRY
Renee Groff

"Cast all your anxieties on him, for he cares about you."
1 Peter 5:7 (RSV)

Sometimes the trials and troubles of life feel like a pile of dirty laundry. You'd rather not deal with it, but you know you can't avoid it, and it just sits there begging for your attention.

I am often too lazy to get the laundry basket to transport my wash from the hamper to the laundry room. So I place a large towel on the floor, pile all the wash in the center, bundle it up and carry it to the washing machine. Occasionally, a stray sock or T-shirt will escape the bundle, so I stop, pick it up and tuck it into the pile.

One day I was lamenting to the Lord about a long list of things that bothered me. Stressful things. Scary things. Unanswered prayers. Long-term situations. I felt like I couldn't focus on the tasks at hand because of all the open-ended problems going on in my life. This was causing sleepless nights and joyless days. As I cried out to the Lord, He gave me a prayer strategy that has been both practical and life-giving as I implemented it in my everyday life.

I felt like the Lord asked me to spread out a towel in my mind, then pile all the things that weighed me down onto the towel, one by one, like dirty laundry.

"God, I give You my children. I give You our finances. I give You my health. I give You my job." I pictured myself laying each situation on the towel as I talked to God about what was bothering me, realizing I had internalized my worries rather than talking to the Lord about them. Even though He already knew what was bothering me, giving voice to my fears and concerns was comforting, knowing He was not just listening but was genuinely concerned for me.

When I had exhausted my list, the Lord asked me to visualize myself wrapping up the towel, just like I do with my laundry, and handing it to Him. Immediately I was reminded of the verse that says, *"Cast all your anxieties on him, for he cares about you"* (1 Peter 5:7). This was it! As silly as it may sound, I found that handing my metaphorical pile of laundry to Him and going about my day freed my mind and heart to think and care about the people and tasks right in front of me.

I've continued this practice on a regular basis. Whenever I find myself overwhelmed and bogged down by multiple things, when the prayer list seems to get longer instead of shorter, I walk through this exercise with the Lord. Sure, sometimes a care or worry seems to slip out of the bundle, just like a sock or T-shirt, and I have to tuck it back in.

The good news? God doesn't seem to mind, and as I hand Him my pile of dirty laundry, I am able to go about my day, knowing He truly does care about me.

Jesus, help me to learn how to trust You to carry my burdens because I can't do it on my own. Increase my faith and teach me how to truly give You my worries and to trust that You care for me. Help me to find rest for my mind and body as I give my concerns to You. Fill me with Your supernatural peace that guards my heart and mind so I can serve You fully and wholeheartedly each day. I declare that You are good, that You are faithful and that Your love for me never fails. In Jesus' Name, Amen.

WITHSTANDING THE WIND
Ashlyn McKayla Ohm

"for you have been my help, and in the shadow of your wings I will sing for joy. My soul clings to you; your right hand upholds me."
Psalm 63:7-8 (ESV)

The wind was rushing through the spring evening. Flowers bowed their heads in surrender as the last dry leaves twirled across the new grass, and the trees flung their branches restlessly. I could even hear slight creaks as my house shuddered against the onslaught.

In the midst of the unsettled landscape, a flash of bright yellow caught my eye. Peering more closely, I noticed that a goldfinch was perched on a limb of the oak tree. With every gust, the branches tossed like ocean waves, buffeting the little goldfinch along with them. Yet the tiny bird didn't look frightened or distressed. Even as it was rocked by the wind, it simply clung tightly to the security of its branch.

I watched this bird, and oh, I felt the conviction.

You see, the wind rises in my life often. An unexpected trial grips me before I ever see it coming. A prayer drenched in tears seems to sink before it reaches the sky. A fear I'd thought was squelched raises its siren song again. And when I feel the "wind," when the branches heave and my faith falters, I panic, certain that I'll tumble to the ground below.

But what if I could adopt the mindset of the little goldfinch?

I'm reminded of Psalm 63. The heading of this psalm denotes it was written by David when he was in the wilderness, evidently hiding from an assassination attempt. Surely during this season in David's life, worry was scratching at his soul. Surely the wind was whipping his security to shreds.

Yet in the midst of the gale, he penned these words of faith to the Lord: *"for you have been my help, and in the shadow of your wings I will sing for joy. My soul clings to you; your right hand upholds me"* (Psalm 63:7-8).

Friend, that's the truth that soothes our souls today. When the wind rises in our lives and it feels as if all is being shaken, God's grace is our security. Does that mean we'll avoid tumult and turmoil? No.

There will still be days when the gale sweeps through every corner of our lives. But when that happens, like the goldfinch, we can respond in faith rather than react in fear. We can choose to view a season of worry only as an opportunity to tighten our grip on God's unshakeable grace. As God was David's help, He is ours today. And safe under the canopy of His wings, we can lift our praise with fearless hearts.

So on the windy days of my life, I see it again in my mind — the sweet face of the trusting goldfinch, safe on the branch and therefore serene in the storm. And I remember: My security isn't threatened by gloomy skies and rising winds. Instead, my security is anchored in Jesus — my hope, help and constant in every gale.

Lord, I confess that when the winds rise, fear is my first impulse. You know that the enemy would love nothing better than to warp my soul with worry. Help me instead to push back the panic and to trust that Your unmovable security is my foundation. Help me cling tightly to Your grace, knowing that Your wings are spread over my soul. And help me live out my trust in You by praising Your name with joy. Tonight, give me the grace to relax in peace, taking a deep breath and resting in Your love. In Jesus' Name, Amen.

YOUR KINGDOM COME
Bethany Fontenot Miller

"Your kingdom come, your will be done, on earth as it is in heaven."
Matthew 6:10 (ESV)

Silent tears cascaded down my face. I'd just received the results from the genetic testing done on our 7-month-old daughter. Her big brown eyes stared up at me, chubby cheeks highlighting her cherub face. How could this vivacious, spirited angel of a baby be anything but perfect?

I'd prayed, believed and hoped those test results would discredit the doctors who told us that a genetic disorder was possible based on some physical abnormalities, but the DNA said differently. Our futures would be filled with numerous medical tests and visits to specialists because of the complications that could come with her diagnosis.

At that moment, I had a decision to make: wallow in grief and self-pity that this was my reality or resolve to entrust my daughter to the One who created her DNA in the first place.

It's difficult to trust. It's hard to relinquish power and surrender authority when the outcome is unknown and the future is uncertain. But perhaps it is even harder to submit that control when you are all too aware of the pain and heartache that the future is capable of bringing. The death of a loved one, a devastating diagnosis, frustrating financial hardships, failed relationships and lost love — all wounds that leave voids not easily mended, regardless of faith.

What did Christ know when He taught us to pray the words, *"Your kingdom come, your will be done, on earth as it is in heaven"* (Matthew 6:10)? He knew that a cross and a grave awaited Him at the end of His earthly ministry. He knew that heartache, rejection, suffering and humiliation marked His future. Of course, the redemption of mankind and a glorious resurrection lay on the other side of the pain and death, but our Bible tells us that Christ's flesh still struggled with drinking that bitter cup. And sometimes, as humans, it's hard or even impossible to see past the suffering and agony of our reality to the purpose of our pain, despite the promises from above.

But, my friend, He knows better than you and me. I may not understand why God does or does not heal my precious baby, but I am confident that He loves her more than I do. I am certain that He holds her and me in the palm of His hand, and I am assured that His Kingdom and His will are worthy to be trusted.

You may have dozens of unanswered questions or pain so raw it takes your breath away. Your hurt may be so deep it feels like you might drown, but trust in this truth: His ways are better than our ways. His thoughts are higher than our thoughts, and His plans are perfect. He does all things well, and His purpose for you is good. He will not waste the pain and suffering you walk through.

Know it, believe it and say it as many times as it takes to convince yourself. His Kingdom over my kingdom. His will above my will. On earth as in heaven.

Lord, I place every worry, fear, disappointment and grief into Your capable hands. Help me to trust that Your way is better than my way. When I don't understand or see the good that can come out of my pain, help me to continue to place my faith in Your will for my life. You are a good Father. You are a faithful Savior, and You know what is best for me. Let Your Kingdom come and Your will be done in me and through me and in my situation. I trust that You know best, O Lord. In Jesus' Name, Amen.

TRADING WORRY FOR PEACE
Julie Bengson

"Rejoice in the Lord always. I will say it again: Rejoice!"
Philippians 4:4 (NIV)

Oh, how I long for a good night's sleep. I lie down and my mind begins to race. It has been two years since I went back to my nursing career. I left a job that I loved, in children's ministry, so I could provide for my family. And we are in the middle of a pandemic with no end in sight. My heart starts to race as tears begin to roll and my chest continues to pound. I try to listen to some worship music, but the thoughts keep coming. I try to read my Bible, but I cannot concentrate. I try to pray, but I cannot find the words.

I put on the worship music again, but this time, I sing the words out loud. I have found that I cannot sing and think at the same time. My heart slowly stops racing, and my chest is no longer pounding. I read Scripture out loud and read my journal, both full of stories of God's amazing grace and mercy. The overwhelming presence of God comes over me, and I feel this amazing calm and peace. Words of praise and thanksgiving flow out of my mouth, and I start to send my prayers to the Father.

Philippians 4:4-9 says, *"Rejoice in the Lord always. I will say it again: Rejoice! Let your gentleness be evident to all. The Lord is near. Do not be anxious about anything, but in every situation, by prayer and petition, with thanksgiving, present your requests to God. And the peace of God, which transcends all understanding, will guard your hearts and your minds in Christ Jesus. Finally, brothers and sisters, whatever is true, whatever is noble, whatever is right, whatever is pure, whatever is lovely, whatever is admirable—if anything is excellent or praiseworthy—think about such things. Whatever you have learned or received or heard from me, or seen in me—put it into practice. And the God of peace will be with you"* (NIV).

What a beautiful verse to remind us God is in control and trustworthy! Therefore, we can give all our worries to Him, and in exchange, He will give us His peace. How do we get this peace?

1.   Rejoice always. God is not asking us to be optimistic or positive all the time. He is asking us to have confidence that He is in control.

2. Be gentle, even-tempered, humble and compassionate toward others. The opposite of being stubborn and demanding our own way.

3. Remember God is always near. We're not alone.

4. Do not be anxious. God does not want us to carry our worries. He wants us to give them all to Him through prayer and petition, giving Him control. Trusting Him fully.

5. Be grateful. Being grateful helps us to remember what God has done in the past and the promises He has fulfilled. This helps us to remember who He is and what He is capable of doing.

6. Focus on whatever is true, noble, right, pure, lovely, admirable, excellent and praiseworthy. What we put in our minds determines what comes out in our words and actions. Fill your mind with the goodness of God.

If we do this, He says His peace will be upon us and with us. True peace is not found in positive thinking, good feelings or the absence of conflict but comes from knowing God is in control. Trade your worries for God's peace and get a good night's sleep tonight.

Heavenly Father, we have confidence that You are in control. We lay down all our worries tonight in exchange for Your peace that surpasses all understanding. We are grateful that You are trustworthy and always keep Your promises. Fill our hearts and minds with more of You. In Jesus' Name, Amen.

THROUGH ABIDING, WE SEE MIRACLES
Amy White

"Abide in Me, and I in you. As the branch cannot bear fruit of itself, unless it abides in the vine, neither can you, unless you abide in Me."
John 15:4 (NKJV)

My tears fell so often; I don't know how I ever managed a smile for my kids. I didn't want them to be as burdened as I felt. My stomach felt hollow. I couldn't eat; nothing appealed to me. I lay awake at night, thinking and dreading morning. Through tearful prayers, I begged God to rescue me or make me *able* to bear up under this burden. I was crumbling to pieces.

In that time of misery, I clung desperately to God. With fragile hope, I tried to trust in God's promises and in His kind, loving character. I wanted a miracle. I needed a miracle.

In Matthew 15, the Bible tells of a crowd of 4,000 needy, hungry people who also needed a miracle. They were desperate. They needed hope and help, so they followed Jesus. They remained with Him for three days as He healed their sick and taught them. Then they ran out of food, and they were hungry. Being far from home, they couldn't easily travel to get food, or they'd risk collapsing. They had a problem with no easy solution in sight.

Friend, can you relate? Are you facing a problem that you can't see a way out of?

Take heart and listen to the rest of this story.

I love this part: Jesus saw them and the problem they faced. Jesus felt compassion for them. (Matthew 15:32) He took what little food they could find among the crowd (seven loaves and a few fish) and gave thanks to God — and as Jesus shared it with the crowd, the food multiplied! *Jesus satisfied their needs,* and there were still seven baskets of food left over. (Matthew 15:37-38) It was a miracle!

After sending the crowd away, Jesus and His disciples went in a boat to another shore, where He was met by the Pharisees, who immediately began arguing with Him, asking for a miracle, testing Him. Jesus refused. (Matthew 16:4)

Do you see who experienced the miracle? The crowd of 4,000 people who remained with Jesus. The phrase "have remained with" is the word *prosmeno* in Greek, with the root word *meno*, which means "to abide." In John 15:4, Jesus tells believers, *"Abide in Me, and I in you. As the branch cannot bear fruit of itself, unless it abides in the vine, neither can you, unless you abide in Me."*

Even though they faced difficulties and discomfort, it was the crowd of people who abided with Jesus who experienced the miracle. The Pharisees saw nothing.

Friend, abiding with Jesus, we see miracles! Abiding with Jesus, our eyes begin to see more clearly how to recognize the Father working in our lives! In my season of tearfully clinging to God, I experienced the miracle of His care through people who encouraged me, shared my burden, helped with my kids, provided meals and prayed. He met me in His Word as He breathed new hope into me. Abiding with Jesus, I experienced His miracles like those 4,000 people did.

The Pharisees were not given a miracle. They missed out by not abiding with Jesus.

Friend, abide with Jesus. As you abide with Him, day after day, remember: He sees you, and His heart feels for you; He will help you. You, my friend, will develop eyes to see the miracles of Jesus in your life as you abide with Him!

Our heavenly Father, thank You for inviting us into an abiding relationship with Jesus where we get to experience His miracles. Help us to trust that You see us, feel for us and will help us. In Jesus' Name, Amen.

A TALE OF TWO PAINTINGS
Hannah Corbett

"He said to them, 'Where is your faith?' And they were afraid, and they marveled, saying to one another, 'Who then is this, that he commands even winds and water, and they obey him?'"
Luke 8:25 (ESV)

Recently I came across a story about a contest to paint a picture of peace.One entry was a beautiful beach on a calm, sunny day. The other was a small family of birds nesting on a cliffside in the middle of a raging storm. The latter won because peace is more than all being well; it's knowing all will be well even in the storms.

A biblical picture of this is when Jesus calmed a storm. The fishermen disciples, who were experienced with the sudden storms on Lake Galilee, were in the middle of one that terrified them. Luke 8:23 says, *"and as they sailed he fell asleep. And a windstorm came down on the lake, and they were filling with water and were in danger"* (ESV).

Afraid for their lives, the disciples woke Jesus up. He immediately stilled the storm. Then, in Luke 8:25, Jesus asked the disciples, *"Where is your faith?"*

The Creator of the wind and waves, God wrapped in human skin, was in the boat with them. There was no reason to be afraid of the storm. That's not easy to swallow when you see waves crashing, the boat breaking, people panicking ... when you see everything except the One in control.

Whatever your situation, if you are a believer in Jesus Christ, He is in the boat with you. There was room for Him to rest in the middle of that storm, and there's room for you to rest in the middle of your storm because He is in the boat.

There's a story about another painting, a real one known as *Checkmate*, showing a defeated-looking man playing chess against Satan. One day a chess grandmaster was staring at it for hours. Then he asked for a chess board and set it up as in the picture. He realized that, whether by accident or design, the man wasn't beaten — his king had one more move. By playing that move, he was able to win the game.

The disciples thought they were drowning when they woke Jesus. How long had they struggled before going to Him? How long had the chess player stared at the board without seeing the king?

Our King can measure the universe with the span of His hand, (Isaiah 40:12) so He's definitely got moves ... and a habit of answering before we even call (Isaiah 65:24)

Our King is personal enough to live inside each of us (1 John 4:4) and able to make all of His grace abound to us so that we have an abundance or every good work. (2 Corinthians 9:8) Let's approach His throne of grace with confidence so that we can receive mercy and find grace to help us in our time of need. (Hebrews 4:16)

Sometimes He wants us to move; sometimes He wants us to act. But sometimes the best thing we can do is be still in the storm and let Him fight for us. (Exodus 14:14)

Where is your faith? Look to the King. He's not done yet. And He's got this.

Lord Jesus, You are the King of kings. You are the Prince of Peace. Thank You that You not only stilled that storm but also rested in the middle of it. I confess: Too many times, I've seen my storms and looked around for help. Help me remember to look at You, to remember Your promise that You've already overcome the trouble I'll have in this world. Help me take hold of Your peace as I let go of my storms and I rest in the knowledge that, however big the waves get, You're still in control. In Jesus' Name, Amen.

RESTORE YOUR CONNECTION
Madison Strausbaugh

*"Know that the L*ORD *has set apart his faithful servant for himself;* *the L*ORD *hears when I call to him."* **Psalm 4:3 (NIV)**

My mom and I often talk on the phone while I am out on a run. As to who does the talking, we swiftly trade back and forth based on the terrain I'm running on, how long I've been running and the content of our conversation. There have been many times when I have done most of the talking and other times when I've breathlessly told her to just keep talking!

On a run in the mountains recently, I hit a dead spot with poor cell signal midstory. "Mom, are you there?"

Nothing.

"Hello?"

Silence.

I quickly picked up my pace, hoping to make my way through the dead zone and restore our connection before I missed too many details or before the call dropped completely.

"Mom, if you can hear me, hold on!"

Actually, it went more like this: "Don't let go, Jack!" She and I often like to quote from *Titanic* when we encounter this problem.

Moments later, our connection was restored. We picked up the conversation near where it had left off, and my pace slowed back down to a comfortable speed as we carried on.

Thankfully, we don't have to be on a run or wearing headphones to be in conversation with God. But have you ever gone through what feels like a dead zone with Him?

Perhaps it feels like you're running through a season of life with poor reception or even a disconnection from God. Maybe you've been silent, or even more likely, you feel like God's been silent.

As I picked up the speed of my run to restore the connection with my mom, I wondered why we don't do the same to restore our connection with God. So often, when the conversation feels silent, we stop talking. We grow weary and slow down. We stop seeking Him and His Word.

But what if we ran faster? What if we kept talking, listened more intently and kept seeking Him no matter what?

When our connection is bad, it's guaranteed that God has not walked away or taken a little vacation — and honestly, I imagine that there is "full coverage" in heaven: 5G, full LTE or whatever is best these days. Psalm 4:3 reassures us that *"the Lord hears when I call to him."*

So it is on our end that the connection grows spotty. Perhaps we've wandered into a place with poor coverage or there is something nearby interfering with our reception.

If you feel disconnected today, I want to encourage you to *run* toward God. Open His Word. Incline your ear in breathlessness. Don't stop talking. He is there. Might there be moments of silence? Yes. But just as my mom remained on the line in the dead zone, God will never hang up.

Do what it takes to restore your connection.

Lord, give me the Psalm 4 assurance of David today. Help me to know and to trust that You hear my prayers. Remind me, Father, that You are working all things for my good and for Your glory. Oh, how often You protect me from myself. Lord, when I feel that You are far from me this week, I will be reminded that You are near. When I feel that You are silent in the days ahead, I will trust in Your timing and rest assured that my prayers have been heard by a loving Father. When our phone line begins to crackle, I will not turn and walk away but run faster to restore our connection. Thank You, Lord, for You are my good, good Father. In Jesus' Name, Amen.

MAKING SENSE OF THE SENSELESS
Kimberly Murray

"'My thoughts are nothing like your thoughts,' says the Lord. 'And my ways are far beyond anything you could imagine.'"
Isaiah 55:8 (NLT)

It's not fair. The thought echoed in my mind again and again, like a throbbing headache I couldn't soothe. My dad had been diagnosed with cancer. I prayed with every ounce of faith I had that God would heal him. I wanted so badly for God to say "yes" to my prayers.

When my dad passed away, I was devastated. My dad was one of the best people you'd ever meet: kind, godly, generous. Why would a good God not heal him? The question plagued me. I felt betrayed and alone.

In the days and weeks that followed, I wrestled with God, trying desperately to make sense of the senseless. One night I was sitting in my car, trying to reconcile what I knew to be true about God with the bitter reality I was walking through. I cried out to God through my tears, "God, I don't understand! Help me understand."

Without a moment's delay, God called to mind Isaiah 55:8: *"'My thoughts are nothing like your thoughts,' says the Lord. 'And my ways are far beyond anything you could imagine.'"*

Those words were the reminder I needed: that even in the wake of the unimaginable, God is still God. And even when I cannot fathom what He is doing or how it could be good, He still has a plan; His plan is still good, and it is not dependent on my understanding.

In that moment I realized I was like a child — unable to grasp why I was being denied the sweet ice cream I so desired and desperately pleaded for. Wondering, *How could a good parent deny me something that is so obviously good?*

It dawned on me that just as a small child would not understand if I explained that the ice cream would keep them up all night and make them cranky the next day, I would not understand if God explained why His answer was "no." Like a child, I have to trust that God is good even when His answer is "no."

"For just as the heavens are higher than the earth, so my ways are higher than your ways and my thoughts higher than your thoughts." (Isaiah 55:9, NLT)

No matter how much I try, I will never fully understand how God works. The good news is — I don't have to. After all, faith is believing what I do not see, trusting what I do not understand.

Sometimes life happens in ways I never expected. Sometimes I wind up with more questions than answers. Sometimes I may wish to demand that God explain Himself. Those feelings are real. But whenever the ache of life's unfairness tempts me to despair or to question God's motives, I remember God knows far more than I do, and in every high and low, He is working for my good.

Tonight I will find rest in knowing I don't have to understand and just letting God hold me. I will remember that the things outside of my reach are never outside of His care.

Father God, tonight You know my heart is aching and my mind is reeling. I can't understand why Your answer to prayer is sometimes "no." But I know You are good even when I don't understand. Help me rest in the knowledge that You know what You're doing, that You love me and have promised never to leave me. Thank You that I don't have to figure You out for You to work things out. May my heart continue to trust in Your sovereign goodness as I rest in Your loving care. In Jesus' Name, Amen.

TRUSTING OUR CREATOR GOD
Cassie Herbert

"For you created my inmost being; you knit me together in my mother's womb. I praise you because I am fearfully and wonderfully made; your works are wonderful, I know that full well."
Psalm 139:13-14 (NIV)

I have a confession. I have a "frenemy" in my life, and his name is The Internet.

As someone who struggles with chronic health issues, The Internet has often seemed like my champion and close confidant. He's helped me locate caring specialists and led me to stories of women on similar journeys. However, at other points, and more frequently if I'm being honest, The Internet has felt like an enemy. He's taunted and teased me down late-night rabbit holes of research in search of answers. He's rocketed my screen time to astronomical numbers as I've gone to him for mindless scrolling and escape.

I do realize the internet isn't an actual person, so why do I so often treat it like one? With every new worry, symptom or potential unknown, my gut response is to reach for my phone and try to Google up some peace of mind! What gives?

The key verses from Psalm 139 made me realize that my "internet problem" was really just a symptom of a greater issue: I had failed to fully trust in God as my sovereign and loving Creator.

"For you created my inmost being; you knit me together in my mother's womb. I praise you because I am fearfully and wonderfully made; your works are wonderful, I know that full well." (Psalm 139:13-14)

God is my Creator. He made me with such intimate love and tender care. As Psalm 139:14 says, *"I am fearfully and wonderfully made."* At this very moment, God knows what is going on with all of my cells, tissues and organs. He even knows how many hairs are on my head! (Luke 12:6-7)

The powerful truth is that when it seems like no one has the answers, my Creator God does. *He knows.*

When I stayed up late searching for answers on the internet, I was trying to take control of something that was never mine to begin with. My search results might have offered temporary relief or peace, but it ultimately lapsed because I'm not all-knowing or all-powerful — only God is. I needed to give control of the unknown back to my Creator.

What a relief we can feel if we realize we no longer have to carry the burden of figuring out all the intricate complexities and mysteries of our bodies! *Our Creator God knows* — and as we submit our worries, questions and pain into His hand, He will direct and guide us in His goodness. (Psalm 23:1-3; Proverbs 3:5-8; 1 Peter 5:6-7; Romans 8:18-31)

I wish I could tell you why you are walking through your current season of struggle and give you a glimpse of how God is working in the unseen. If I could grab your hand in this moment, I would, and we could tenderly encourage each other to trust. Trust our loving Creator who sees us and loves us. Trust that He knows the pain we are carrying in our minds, hearts and bodies. Trust that He will lead us through — He will not abandon His beloved creations.

Dear heavenly Father, thank You that You created me with such love and care. Remind me that You see me and know the inner workings of my body, even when it seems like no one else does. Help me to find reassurance and peace in that truth. Quiet my mind and give me peaceful rest tonight. In Jesus' Name, Amen.

ACKNOWLEDGEMENTS

Proverbs 31 Ministries and COMPEL Writers Training would like to offer a special thanks to the talented devotion writers featured in this book, all of whom are members of COMPEL Writers Training. Their devotions were chosen out of almost 500 submissions in a COMPEL devotion-writing challenge. Writers, we congratulate and applaud you

for your hard work and dedication to your craft of writing and for bravely offering your words of truth and encouragement to the world. You are touching hearts and lives in ways you will never understand until eternity. Keep up the good work, faithful servants!

"You are the light of the world. A town built on a hill cannot be hidden. Neither do people light a lamp and put it under a bowl. Instead they put it on its stand, and it gives light to everyone in the house. In the same way, let your light shine before others, that they may see your good deeds and glorify your Father in heaven." (Matthew 5:14-16, NIV)

ABOUT PROVERBS 31 MINISTRIES

Know the Truth. Live the Truth. It changes everything.

If you were inspired by this devotional and desire to deepen your own personal relationship with Jesus Christ, Proverbs 31 Ministries has just what you are looking for.

Proverbs 31 Ministries exists to be a trusted friend who will take you by the hand and walk by your side, leading you one step closer to the heart of God through:

- Free online daily devotions.
- First 5 Bible study app.
- Online Bible Studies.
- *The Proverbs 31 Ministries Podcast.*
- COMPEL Writers Training.
- She Speaks Conference.
- Books and resources.

Our desire is to help you to know the Truth and live the Truth. Because when you do, it changes everything.

For more information about Proverbs 31 Ministries, visit proverbs31.org.

  @proverbs31ministries

JOIN COMPEL WRITERS TRAINING

COMPEL Writers Training is a faith-based
online writers training community.

**GROW IN YOUR CALLING AS A WRITER
BY JOINING COMPEL, WHERE YOU WILL:**

- Receive insider training from Lysa TerKeurst and
  other bestselling authors who know the publishing
  industry inside out.

- Learn how to overcome the challenges you face as
  a writer, so you can accomplish your writing goals.

- Gain access to publishing opportunities not
  found anywhere else, which can help your writing
  dreams come true.

Whether you are just starting to write or need to figure
out your next move, COMPEL can help you identify the
next steps and equip you to take them.

*Learn more and sign up for just $35 a month
at compeltraining.com.*

f 📷 @compeltraining

ENCOURAGEMENT FOR TODAY DEVOTIONS

Do you want to know and live the Truth of God's Word but need daily reminders to help you?

Encouragement for Today devotions are free daily devotions sent straight to your inbox. Whether you're looking for guidance in your faith, friendships, family, marriage, relationships, workplace or neighborhood, our writers combine God's Truth with compassionate insight and practical application.

Go to proverbs31.org/read/devotions to sign up for *free!*